Making Sense of Federal Dollars:

A Funding Guide for Social Service Providers

by Madelyn DeWoody

Child Welfare League of America, Washington, DC

CHILD WELFARE LEAGUE OF AMERICA, INC.
440 First Street, NW, Suite 310
Washington, DC 20001-2085

CURRENT PRINTING (last digit)
10 9 8 7 6 5 4 3 2 1

Cover and text design by Paul Butler

Printed in the United States of America

ISBN # 0–87868–505–7

Contents

Preface

Hard times are forcing public and nonprofit agencies to expand their thinking about how to fund services for children, youths, and families. Clients' needs are becoming increasingly complex and demanding more intensive and more integrated services. At the same time, state and local funding is being constricted, presenting funding challenges for public and nonprofit agencies that serve children, youths, and families.

Fortunately, both public and nonprofit agencies are discovering the multiple funding options available through federal funding streams. Through creative and innovative thinking, agencies can access federal dollars to finance child welfare services, health care, mental health and substance abuse treatment services, educational and developmental services, and child day care. These strategies are particularly effective when developed through a cooperative partnership between the public and private sectors.

This guide gives social service providers basic information on a range of federal funding programs. Specifically targeted to providers who serve children and families, it provides an overview of each program so that providers may educate themselves and their clients about the benefits and opportunities available under a variety of federal programs to address the needs of vulnerable children, youths, and families.

Section I
Medicaid

An essential element in any overview of federal funding for enhancing and expanding services to children and families is Medicaid, the federal/state-financed program of medical assistance for low-income persons. Enacted in 1965 as an amendment to the Social Security Act, Medicaid comprises Title XIX of that act and, over the last three decades, has become a significant factor in the financing and delivery of a wide array of health services to low-income children and families.

The laws surrounding Medicaid have been described by some courts as "almost unintelligible to the uninitiated,"[1] "among the most intricate ever drafted by Congress,"[2] and "an aggravated assault on the English language, resistant to attempts to understand it."[3] This complexity stems from the numerous federal statutory requirements, regulations, and guidelines that govern the program along with a variety of state laws, regulations, and guidelines designed to implement the program in each state.

Despite its complexity, Medicaid can be distilled into several major categories of rules that drive the program. This section focuses on Medicaid law and policy in the areas of administration, eligibility, service delivery, and provider qualifications, and considers these issues from the perspective of agencies that serve children and families.

1. *Friedman v. Berger*, 547 F.2d 724, 727, n. 7 (2d Cir. 1976).
2. *Schweiker v. Gray Panthers*, 453 U.S. 34, 43 (1981).
3. *Feld v. Berger*, 424 F. Supp. 1356, 1357 (S.D.N.Y. 1976).

Chapter 1
The Administration
of Medicaid

Medicaid: A Summary

Nature of Program
Medicaid is a federal-state program that funds health care services to poor and low-income persons. Eligibility for Medicaid and Medicaid-covered services is determined by federal law, with some discretion left to the states. States are required to provide Medicaid-eligible children with screening, diagnosis, and treatment services through the Early and Periodic Screening, Diagnosis, and Treatment Program (EPSDT).
Funding Type
Federal entitlement.
For More Information
Medicaid Bureau, HCFA-DHHS, East High Rise Building, Room 233, 6325 Security Boulevard, Baltimore, MD 21207. Phone: 410/966–3870 or 202/690–5636.

The Federal-State Partnership

Medicaid is a joint federal/state program that provides medical assistance to low-income children, youths, and families. At the federal level, the Health Care Financing Administration (HCFA) of the United States Department of Health and Human Services (HHS) has responsibility for both Medicaid and Medicare. At the state level, states are given broad latitude, within certain federal parameters, to develop a plan to provide Medicaid services within their borders.* Each state must designate a single state agency as responsible for Medicaid. Because of the flexibility that states have in implementing the program, the nature and scope of the Medicaid program varies considerably from one state to another and a variety of agencies may have Medicaid responsibility. Table 1 illustrates the types of state agencies designated to administer or oversee Medicaid.

The State Medicaid Plan
Plan Approval
A state's Medicaid plan is essentially a contract between the state and HCFA, which administers the Medicaid program. The plan outlines the services the state will provide under the Medicaid program, who will be covered, and how the program will operate.

HCFA must approve each state's plan. If a state later chooses to add services to its plan or serve new groups of individuals through Medicaid, it must amend the plan. Some states require legislative approval of amendments to their Medicaid plans, but most amend their plans administratively. HCFA regional offices, which operate throughout the United States, must approve amendments to the Medicaid plans of states within each region. Although the HCFA regional office usually approves state plan amendments, in instances when an amendment is not approved, the state has an automatic right to appeal to the central HCFA office and to federal court if the HCFA central office withholds approval.

Plan Requirements
In designing their Medicaid programs, states must generally meet requirements on amount, duration, and scope of services; comparability; statewideness; and freedom of choice.

Amount, Duration, and Scope of Services. Services for each category of persons that the state serves under its Medicaid plan must be sufficient in amount, duration, and scope to reason-

Table 1. Types of Designated State Agencies

Designated State Agency	Number of States
▪ Welfare/social service department	25
▪ Health department	4
▪ Combined health/social service department	15
▪ Independent entity	4
▪ Larger agency other than health or social services	2
▪ Combination of state and local agencies jointly administering program	6

*The term state will be used in the pages that follow to include not only the 50 states, but also the District of Columbia and the other jurisdictions listed in table 3, including American Samoa, Guam, the Northern Mariana Islands, Puerto Rico, and the Virgin Islands. The Bureau of Indian Affairs under the U.S. Secretary of the Interior is also considered a state for some purposes.

ably achieve the purpose of the service. A state, for example, could not limit the number of days of inpatient hospital care it covered under Medicaid to two days a year, as such a limitation would in many cases prevent the hospitalization from achieving its purpose.

Comparability. Comparability focuses on equitable coverage of services among Medicaid recipients. The services made available to any categorically needy Medicaid beneficiary in the state must be equal in amount, scope, and duration to those available to any other categorically needy beneficiary in the state. The same rule applies to beneficiaries within any covered medically needy group. A state, for example, could not provide family planning services to some categorically needy Medicaid recipients and not to others.

Comparability, however, does not have to be met under the Early and Periodic Screening, Diagnosis, and Treatment (EPSDT) program (the health screening and treatment program for children under the age of 21); targeted case management services; or home-and community-based waivers. These exceptions are described in greater detail later in this section.

Statewideness. Generally, a state's Medicaid plan must be in effect throughout the entire state. Exceptions exist, however. Targeted case management services, with HCFA approval, may be provided to a specific geographic area within the state. Likewise, home- and community-based waiver programs do not have to meet the statewideness requirement. These exceptions are described in greater detail later in this section.

Freedom of Choice. Under a state's Medicaid plan, Medicaid beneficiaries must be allowed to obtain services from any provider who provides Medicaid-covered services and is a qualified provider with regard to those services. This requirement, however, may be expressly waived by HCFA under a freedom-of-choice waiver.

Federal Financial Participation

Although the federal government shares the costs of the Medicaid program with state governments, the federal payment (Federal Financial Participation or FFP) differs for various Medicaid activities. Table 2 provides the FFP for each type of Medicaid activity.

The federal matching rate (Federal Medical Assistance Percentage or FMAP) determines the share of dollars the federal government will pay for Medicaid services. FMAP is determined through a statutory formula that takes into account the state's per capita income in relation to the national per capita income. Under Medicaid law, the minimum FMAP is 50 percent of the costs of the services; the maximum is 83 percent. Table 3 provides the FMAP rates for Medicaid services that are in effect for each state and jurisdiction for FY 1994.

The State Match

States and jurisdictions use a variety of mechanisms to generate funds to pay for their portion of Medicaid expenditures. Three such mechanisms have been subject to close examination by HCFA and the Office of Management and Budget (OMB).

On December 12, 1991, after a multi-year struggle among HCFA/OMB, Congress, and the states, the Medicaid Moratorium Amendments (P.L. 102–234) were signed into law, setting forth rules to govern the mechanisms for generating the state match.

Voluntary Contributions. Prior to the amendments, voluntary contributions to the state included privately donated funds, often from hospitals, that the state used as part of its Medicaid match. They also included the donation of on-site office space to Medicaid eligibility workers who were outstationed, that is, working from locations other than public welfare offices (i.e., hospitals and clinics). Under the 1991 amendments, however, after October 1992, most donated funds are no longer permitted for purposes of generating the state's share of Medicaid costs. The only acceptable provider donations will be: (1) "bona fide provider-related donations" (donations for which there is no link between the donation and the provided service), and (2) eligibility worker training and outstationing. Contribu-

tions for outstationed enrollment administrative activities are capped at 10 percent of a state's Medicaid program total administrative expenses.

Provider-Specific Taxes. These taxes generally are placed on hospital revenues to generate state matching funds. Under the 1991 amendments, states may continue to use special taxes but they must be uniform, must apply to an entire class of items or services, and must be imposed with respect to all items and services furnished by all nonfederal, nonpublic providers in the state. Such taxes may not generate more than 25 percent of the state's share of Medicaid. States already above the 25 percent level may continue to cover the proportion of state share already financed through such taxes. The 25 percent tax cap will terminate in 1995.

Intergovernmental Transfers. The use of local and state funds, transferred between local and state governments and among state agencies, may be continued as long as the practice does not violate the restrictions on voluntary contributions and provider-specific taxes set forth in the 1991 amendments.

Table 2. Federal Financial Participation

Medicaid Activity	Federal Financial Participation
■ Expenditures for Medicaid Services	Between 50% and 83% depending upon the state's per capita income (see table 3)
■ Administrative costs	50% (all states)
■ Compensation and training of skilled professional medical personnel in program administration	75% (all states)
■ Costs of offering, arranging, and providing family planning services and supplies	90% (all states)
■ Expenditures for services through Indian Health Services facilities	100% (all states)

Table 3. Federal Medical Assistance Percentages (FY 1994)

State	Federal Medical Assistance Percentages	State	Federal Medical Assistance Percentages
Alabama	71.22	Montana	71.05
Alaska	50.00	Nebraska	61.96
American Samoa	50.00	Nevada	50.31
Arizona	65.90	New Hampshire	50.00
Arkansas	74.46	New Jersey	50.00
California	50.00	New Mexico	74.17
Colorado	54.30	New York	50.00
Connecticut	50.00	North Carolina	65.14
Delaware	50.00	North Dakota	71.13
District of Columbia	50.00	Northern Mariana	50.00
Florida	54.76	Ohio	60.83
Georgia	62.47	Oklahoma	70.39
Guam	50.00	Oregon	62.12
Hawaii	50.00	Pennsylvania	54.61
Idaho	70.92	Puerto Rico	50.00
Illinois	50.00	Rhode Island	53.87
Indiana	63.49	South Carolina	71.08
Iowa	63.33	South Dakota	69.50
Kansas	59.52	Tennessee	67.15
Kentucky	70.91	Texas	64.18
Louisiana	73.49	Utah	74.35
Maine	61.96	Vermont	59.55
Maryland	50.00	Virgin Islands	50.00
Massachusetts	50.00	Virginia	50.00
Michigan	56.37	Washington	54.24
Minnesota	54.65	West Virginia	75.72
Mississippi	78.85	Wisconsin	60.47
Missouri	60.64	Wyoming	65.63

Chapter 2
Medicaid Eligibility, Services, and Providers

It is helpful to approach Medicaid law as a series of rules that answer three major questions: (1) Who is eligible for Medicaid?; (2) What services are covered under Medicaid?; and (3) Who are the qualified providers of Medicaid services?

Who is Eligible for Medicaid?

Eligibility for Medicaid was originally tied to eligibility for public welfare benefits (i.e., Aid to Families with Dependent Children (AFDC) and the Supplemental Security Income (SSI) Program). Medicaid eligibility requirements, however, have evolved from their historic link with cash assistance programs to incorporate other groups of individuals. Primarily, eligibility has been expanded to pregnant women and their children, who now may qualify for Medicaid at income levels that previously would have disqualified them. To be eligible for Medicaid, individuals must fit within one of three major categories:

1. *The categorically needy.* Some individuals in this group must be covered under Medicaid; others may be covered at state option.

2. *SSI recipients.* The eligibility of members of this group varies by state.

3. *The medically needy.* States may choose to cover individuals with

incomes above the ceiling for Medicaid but with substantial medical expenses.

If an individual meets a state's eligibility criteria and resides in that state, the state must provide Medicaid coverage, even if the individual does not have a fixed or permanent address. Each state must develop mechanisms to ensure that documentation establishing Medicaid eligibility is available to persons who do not have a permanent home or mailing address.

The Categorically Needy

While certain groups of individuals must be covered under Medicaid, other groups may be covered under a state's Medicaid plan at the state's option. *Mandatory Coverage.* Categories of individuals who must be covered under every state's Medicaid plan include:

- Individuals who are eligible for AFDC benefits (see chapter 7);

- Children who are eligible for Title IV-E foster care or adoption assistance payments (see chapter 4);

- Pregnant women and their children to the age of six with household incomes up to 133 percent of the poverty line;

- Infants born to Medicaid-eligible mothers as long as the infant is in the mother's home and the mother continues to be eligible for Medicaid or would be eligible for Medicaid if she were pregnant; and

- Through a phase-in process to be completed in the year 2002, all children up to age 19 who were born after September 30, 1983, and who are in

families with incomes at or below 100 percent of the federal poverty line.

Optional Coverage. A state may choose to extend categorically needy coverage to additional groups, sometimes referred to as the *optional categorically needy.* Individuals who qualify as optional categorically needy are automatically eligible for all Medicaid-covered services specified in the state's plan. By contrast, those qualifying for Medicaid as *medically needy* (discussed below) usually have access to a more limited range of Medicaid services. Groups that a state may choose to cover as optional categorically needy include:

1. *Near-poor pregnant women and their infants.* States have the option of extending Medicaid coverage to pregnant women and their children up to one year of age with incomes up to 185 percent of the federal poverty line.

2. *Ribicoff children.* This group of children is named for former U.S. Senator Abraham Ribicoff, who sponsored legislation authorizing the coverage of children up to age 21 who are not within the mandated categories of recipients that a state must cover. A state may cover all children in this category or it may create "reasonable categories" of children who would be eligible for benefits under AFDC if the children met the AFDC definition of dependency (i.e., children in certain two-parent households). Examples of "reasonable categories" that states have established under the Ribicoff option are children in privately subsidized out-of-home care and children in certain institutional settings. This

category has been used by many states to extend Medicaid coverage to children who are not eligible for Title IV-E foster care maintenance payments but who are in family foster care, group care, or residential treatment.

3. *Children under certain adoption assistance agreements.* In addition to providing Medicaid coverage to certain children covered under Title IV-E adoption assistance agreements, a state may cover children for whom non-Title IV-E adoption assistance agreements are in effect if (1) the state determines that the child has special needs, and (2) the child would have been eligible for Medicaid prior to the time that the adoption assistance agreement was completed.

4. *The Katie Beckett option.* This optional category of coverage under Medicaid extends to certain noninstitutionalized disabled children who, under the usual financial eligibility rules, would not be eligible for Medicaid if they lived at home. Under general Medicaid eligibility rules, a child who lives at home has some portion of his or her parent's

income "deemed" as the child's income in determining eligibility for Medicaid. Such deeming of income does not occur if the child is in an institution. Under the Katie Beckett option, a state does not deem the parent's income to the child living at home if four conditions are met:

• The child is 18 years old or younger and would be eligible for Medicaid if institutionalized.

• The child requires a level of care equivalent to the state's criteria for hospital care, nursing home care, or care in an intermediate care facility for the mentally retarded.

• The child can be appropriately cared for outside an institutional setting.

• The estimated cost of care at home is no greater than the estimated cost of institutional care.

If these criteria are met, a child with disabilities who ordinarily would be eligible for Medicaid only if institutionalized may qualify for Medicaid while being cared for at home.

Tables 4 and 5 summarize the rules that govern categorical eligibility for

Table 4. 1994 Poverty Guidelines

Size of Family Unit	Alaska	Hawaii	All Other States and the District of Columbia
1	$9,206	$8,470	$7,360
2	12,300	11,320	9,840
3	15,400	14,170	12,320
4	18,500	17,020	14,800
5	21,600	19,870	17,280
6	24,700	22,720	19,760
7	27,800	25,570	22,240
8	30,900	28,420	24,720

Medicaid. Table 4 provides the 1994 poverty guidelines used to calculate Medicaid eligibility. Table 5 summarizes the eligibility rules by income for various groups of pregnant women and for children.

Children who are eligible for Supplemental Security Income (SSI) (see chapter 6) may also be eligible for Medicaid. States have the option of treating the SSI/Medicaid relationship in one of three ways:

1. A child who is eligible for SSI is automatically enrolled in Medicaid. Thirty-one states and the District of Columbia follow this option.

2. A child who is eligible for SSI is automatically eligible for Medicaid but must complete a separate Medicaid application. Seven states follow this option: Alaska, Idaho, Kansas, Nebraska, Nevada, Oregon, and Utah.

3. A child who is eligible for SSI must apply separately for Medicaid, for which eligibility is determined under standards that are different from SSI eligibility

standards. Twelve states follow this option. Three of these states—Indiana, Missouri, and New Hampshire—have stricter criteria for determining disability for Medicaid purposes than those used for SSI disability determinations. Nine states—Connecticut, Illinois, Minnesota, North Dakota, Oklahoma, Hawaii, North Carolina, Ohio, and Virginia—use the same definition of disability but employ stricter financial criteria for determining Medicaid eligibility than those used for SSI.

The Medically Needy

States may also choose to extend Medicaid coverage to individuals other than those the program mandates by covering a defined group of medically needy persons in their plans. The *medically needy* are persons who (1) except for income and resources, fall into one of the categories covered by the state in its Medicaid plan, such as the aged, blind, disabled, families with dependent children, or pregnant women and their children; and (2) have income

Table 5. Medicaid Coverage of Pregnant Women and Children, Based on Federal Poverty Level (FPL)

Designated State Agency	100% FPL	133% FPL	185% FPL
Pregnant women	Mandatory	Mandatory	Optional
Children up to 12 months	Mandatory	Mandatory	Optional
Children 12 months to 6 years	Mandatory	Mandatory	Not covered
Children 6 years to 19 years	Mandatory phase-in for all children born after 9/30/83	Not covered	Not covered

and/or resources that are within the medically needy standards established by the state—standards that are higher than the income standards set for categorically needy coverage.

Under these provisions, an individual who does not qualify for AFDC or SSI because his or her income is too high may, nevertheless, become eligible for Medicaid through "spend down" provisions, under which medical expenses are subtracted to reduce income to a level comparable to the AFDC income threshold. A state that has a program for the medically needy must, at a minimum, provide coverage to children and pregnant women who would be eligible as mandatory categorically needy but who have income and resources in excess of permitted levels for categorical eligibility. Table 6 lists the states and jurisdictions that have opted to cover the medically needy within their Medicaid plans.

The Eligibility Determination Process

The eligibility determination process for Medicaid has historically taken place at the same locations where applications for AFDC are taken, usually at public welfare offices. In 1990, Congress mandated that, effective July 1, 1991, the Medicaid application process include the outstationing of eligibility workers. At a minimum, eligibility workers are to be outstationed on a full-time basis at disproportionate share hospitals, federally qualified health centers, and clinics that treat significant numbers of low-income women, infants, and children. All costs associated with the outstationing application process, including salary and equipment costs, are reimbursed by the federal government at the 50 percent administrative matching rate.

In its 1990 legislation, Congress also addressed the cumbersome and

Table 6. States and Jurisdictions with Programs for the Medically Needy, as of October 1, 1992*

American Samoa	Hawaii	Michigan	Northern Mariana Islands	Texas
Arkansas	Illinois	Minnesota	Oklahoma	Utah
California	Iowa	Montana	Oregon	Vermont
Connecticut	Kansas	Nebraska	Pennsylvania	Virgin Islands
District of Columbia	Kentucky	New Hampshire	Puerto Rico	Virginia
Florida	Louisiana	New Jersey	Rhode Island	Washington
Georgia	Maine	New York	South Carolina	West Virginia
	Maryland	North Carolina	Tennessee	Wisconsin
	Massachusetts	North Dakota		

*As reported in Committee on Ways and Means, U.S. House of Representatives, *1993 Green Book* (Washington, DC: U.S. Government Printing Office, 1993).

complex nature of Medicaid application forms, and their frequent combination with the equally intricate AFDC application. The 1990 legislation mandates that a short-form Medicaid application be used at all outstation sites and that states develop forms that contain only the information necessary to determine Medicaid eligibility (i.e., verification of pregnancy, children's ages, family size, family income, and lawful U.S. residence). HCFA, however, has not required states to develop a short-form application, but has allowed them the option of using pre-existing multiprogram applications, provided that the person assisting the Medicaid applicant obtains only the information that is pertinent to Medicaid eligibility. Most states have chosen to rely on some form of multiprogram application rather than streamlining the Medicaid application form as federal legislators anticipated.

What Services are Covered under Medicaid?

Medicaid provides coverage for services that are defined as *medical assistance* under section 1905(a) of the Social Security Act. Although a state may choose to include a service in its Medicaid plan that is not listed in federal medical law, federal financial assistance is available only if the service falls within one of the statutory medical assistance service definitions.

Some Medicaid-covered services must be covered by a state under its Medicaid plan. Table 7 lists the core services that states are required to offer to all categorically needy individuals.

Somewhat different rules regarding mandatory services apply for individuals eligible for Medicaid as medically needy.

1. States may choose to provide the medically needy with the same services offered to the categorically needy.

Table 7. Mandatory Medicaid Services

- Inpatient hospital services

- Outpatient hospital services

- Rural health clinic services

- Laboratory and X-ray services

- Skilled nursing facility (SNF) services for individuals 21 year or older

- Early and periodic screening, diagnosis, and treatment (EPSDT) for individuals under 21 years of age

- Physicians' services

- Home health services for any individual entitled to SNF care

- Nurse midwife services (to the extent that nurse midwives are authorized to practice under state law)

- Family planning services and supplies

2. At a minimum, the following services must be offered:

- Ambulatory services to children under the age of 18;

- The same package of services provided to categorically needy pregnant women; and

- Home health services to those entitled to nursing care under the state's medically needy program.

3. A state may not offer services to the medically needy that are not also available to the categorically needy.

Mandatory Services: EPSDT

One of the most important mandatory Medicaid service is the Early and Periodic Screening, Diagnosis, and Treatment (EPSDT) program. EPSDT must be provided to all categorically needy children under the age of 21. When a state has opted to extend Medicaid coverage to a defined "medically needy" population, it has the option of providing EPSDT for that group. If a state elects to provide the EPSDT benefit for the medically needy, however, EPSDT must be made available to all Medicaid-eligible children under age 21.

EPSDT, as designed by Congress, is intended to function as a gateway to the provision of a broad array of health care screening and treatment services for Medicaid-eligible children. It has two major components: screening, and follow-up diagnosis and treatment for conditions, problems, and defects that have been identified through screening.

EPSDT Screening. The EPSDT program screens children to uncover physical challenges, mental health problems, developmental conditions, and dental needs.

Periodic Screening. Screening must occur on a "periodic" basis. States are required to establish screening schedules for children at intervals that meet standards of reasonable medical and dental practice as determined by the state after consultation with recognized medical and dental organizations involved in child health care. The state must develop separate "periodicity" schedules for vision, hearing, dental care, and general health screenings. The periodic visit schedules must assure at least a minimum number of physical, mental health, and developmental health examinations and behavioral assessments at critical points in the child's life. For example, developmental and behavioral assessments for infants should take place at one month, two months, four months, six months, nine months, and one year. At a minimum, screening must include: (1) a comprehensive health and developmental history that includes assessment of both physical and mental health development; (2) a comprehensive physical examination; (3) appropriate immunizations according to age or health history; (4) laboratory tests, which may include assessment of lead level in the blood based on age and risk factors; and (5) health education, including counseling for parents and children.

Under HCFA guidelines for EPSDT screens, assessments for developmental problems must include motor development, language development, self-help skills, and social-emotional development and cognitive skills. For adolescents, screenings should encompass learning disabilities, peer relations, psychological/psychiatric problems, and problems involving dependence on alcohol and other drugs. The guidelines recognize that screening for issues common to adolescents, such as psychosocial and emotional status, chemical dependency, and reproductive health, may necessitate health supervision at more frequent intervals than the generally recommended two- to three-year period.

EPSDT screening services do not have to be provided to Medicaid-eligible adults, nor do they have to be provided outside of the EPSDT program. Children who are Medicaid eligible are entitled to health screenings through EPSDT whether or not such screenings are provided to individuals 21 years or older.

Interperiodic Screening. Under current law, interperiodic screens also must be reimbursed under Medicaid. States must allow screens between the screening intervals established under the periodic schedules when the need arises. If a physical or mental illness or condition is suspected, the child must be provided a screen when it is medically necessary to diagnose the problem. For example, a child may have been screened for vision and no abnormality detected. If the child then enters a preschool program and the teacher suspects a vision problem, the child would be entitled to an interperiodic vision screen to reevaluate his

or her vision.

Partial Screening. States may use partial screens to assess and identify specific aspects of the child's health and development. Some states have utilized partial screens to identify mental health and developmental problems when the initial, more comprehensive screen indicates a potential problem in one of those areas. Table 8 lists some of the states that utilize partial screens under EPSDT.

EPSDT Treatment Services. Amendments to the Social Security Act contained in the Omnibus Budget Reconciliation Act (OBRA) of 1989 expanded the treatment requirements of EPSDT. EPSDT must now cover diagnostic and treatment services that are medically necessary to remedy defects, illnesses, and conditions identified in screenings. When a screening identifies a physical or mental defect, illness, or condition, states must now provide, under Medicaid, all treatment and follow-up services listed in Medicaid law if they are medically necessary, regardless of whether such services are otherwise included in the state's Medicaid plan. Consequently, although a service may be optional and a state may not provide the service under its Medicaid plan to all Medicaid eligible individuals, it becomes a mandated service for a particular child when the EPSDT screen identifies a defect, illness, or condition for which the service is medically necessary. EPSDT benefits also include certain case management services, such as assistance with scheduling appointments or transportation, to ensure that children receive the benefits of comprehensive health care. As of May, 1994, the regulations governing these changes in the EPSDT program had not been issued in final form, and state implementation of the statutory changes has been uneven. Lawsuits have been brought in some states in an attempt to expedite state compliance with statutory requirements.

It is important to emphasize that Medicaid-eligible children and youths served by child-caring agencies are entitled to receive any Medicaid-coverable service that is medically necessary to correct a diagnosed defect, illness, or condition, *even if other Medicaid beneficiaries are not entitled to receive those services in the state.* Federal law requires that the amount, scope, and duration of EPSDT services be sufficient to reasonably achieve the purposes for which those services are provided. This mandate ensures that treatment and follow-up services are adequate to correct or remedy the child's problems. Federal law also requires that a service under EPSDT not be denied arbitrarily or reduced solely because of the diagnosis, type of illness, or condition.

Figure 1 illustrates the relationships among the types of screens available under EPSDT screening, follow-up diagnosis, and treatment services. *Other Services.* States are also required to assist EPSDT-eligible children with other services. Those services include transportation when necessary and requested and other requested support services, such as assistance in scheduling appointments. *EPSDT Providers.* The current interim regulations that govern EPSDT expressly direct states to make maximum use of all available providers for

Table 8. States Using EPSDT Partial Screens

Type of Partial Screen	States Developing/Using
Developmental assessment with a separate EPSDT screening code	Connecticut Michigan Nevada Maine
Developmental assessment and unclothed physical examination with separate EPSDT screening codes	Arkansas Maryland Missouri
Mental health assessment with separate EPSDT screening code	New Mexico
Single, multipurpose code for all EPSDT partial screens	California Kentucky

EPSDT screening and treatment services. States are encouraged to broadly expand the provider base to ensure access to services. EPSDT screening may be performed by any Medicaid-enrolled physician, dentist, or other provider qualified under state law to furnish primary medical and health care services. Screening sites may include community health centers, school health programs, and Head Start centers. States may not limit EPSDT screening or treatment services to providers having exclusive contracts to perform EPSDT services. Likewise, states may not limit EPSDT providers to agencies only in the private sector or only in the public sector.

EPSDT Enrollment. States are required to achieve an EPSDT partici-

pation rate of 80 percent by the year 1995—that is, they must ensure that 80 percent of Medicaid-eligible children to age 21 have received EPSDT screens. Interim goals have been set for each year to ensure that progress is being made in increasing the number of children enrolled in EPSDT and that the 80 percent goal will be achieved.

States are also required to inform families about the availability and benefits of EPSDT and must enroll children in EPSDT within 60 days of determination of Medicaid eligibility. Additionally, any Medicaid eligible child who requests EPSDT services from a provider is entitled to receive them.

Optional Services. In addition to the mandated services, states may offer a

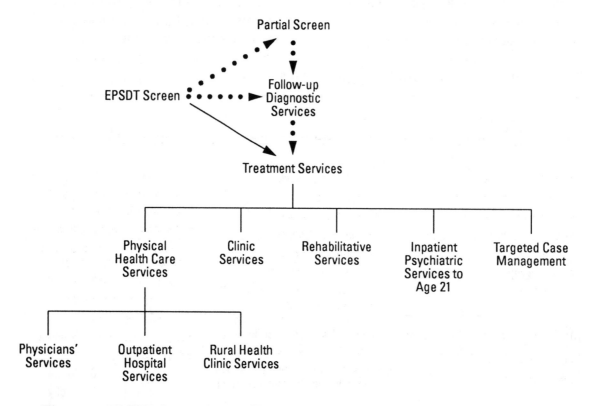

Figure 1. EPSDT Screening, Follow-up Diagnosis, and Treatment Services

broad range of other services as part of their Medicaid plans. There are more than 30 optional service categories, each carrying federal matching funds, that states may include in their Medicaid plans. Because states are free to select from the various optional services permitted under Medicaid law and to define those services, the type and scope of the benefits offered to individuals eligible for Medicaid varies substantially among the states. Table 9 lists the optional services states may include in their Medicaid plans.

The state's Medicaid plan provides information on whether a state has selected an optional service and how the state defines the scope of that service. States have considerable latitude in defining the nature and scope of particular optional services, setting the medical necessity criteria that determine recipient access to the service, and crafting utilization control procedures, such as prior authorization, that may be used to determine coverage in a particular case.

Several optional services under Medicaid are of particular relevance to the children, youths, and families social service agencies serve. These Medicaid service categories have been used by some states to refinance services that traditionally have not been covered by Medicaid but have been funded through other sources. Clinic services, rehabilitative services, targeted case management, inpatient psychiatric services to individuals through age 21, and transportation services are service categories that have been creatively used by states to broaden services to children, youths, and families under the Medicaid program. Table 10 summarizes the Medicaid services most relevant to providers who serve children and families.

Clinic Services. Federal law broadly defines *clinic services* as encompass-

Table 9. Optional Medicaid Services

- Podiatrists' services
- Optometrists' services
- Chiropractors' services
- Other practitioners' services
- Private duty nursing services
- Clinic services
- Dental services
- Occupational services
- Services for speech, hearing, and language disorders
- Prescribed drugs
- Dentures

- Prosthetic devices
- Eyeglasses
- Diagnostic services
- Screening services
- Preventive services
- Rehabilitative services
- Services for individuals age 65 or older in mental institutions (inpatient hospitals), skilled nursing facilities; and intermediate care facilities)
- Intermediate care facility services for the mentally retarded

- Inpatient psychiatric services for individuals under age 22
- Christian Science nurses
- Christian Science sanitariums
- Skilled nursing facilities for individuals under age 21
- Emergency hospital services
- Personal care services
- Transportation services
- Case management services
- Hospice services

ing any preventive, diagnostic, therapeutic, or rehabilitative service furnished to outpatients. Clinic services must be provided in a facility that is not a hospital but is organized and operated to provide care to outpatients. Because of this requirement, clinic services are "on-site" services: they must be provided at the provider's facility. Exception to the on-site requirement is made only when clinic services are provided to individuals who are homeless. In addition, clinic services must be furnished by or under the direction of a physician or dentist.

Clinic services are primarily based on a medical model, and states generally have followed that model in developing them. States that have chosen to include

Table 10. Medicaid Services: A Comparison

Service	Early and Periodic Screening, Diagnosis, and Treatment	Clinic Services	Rehabilitative Services	Targeted Case Management	Inpatient Psychiatric Services Through Age 21	Transportation Services
Type	Mandatory	Optional*	Optional*	Optional*	Optional*	Optional*/**
Nature	Screening and follow-up diagnosis and treatment	Medically directed mental health and health services	Medical or psychosocial therapeutic services	Case assessment, coordination, tracking, and monitoring	Therapeutic services and room and board	Necessary transportation for care
Eligible Group	To age 21	Children and/or adults	Children and/or adults	As defined in state plan	Through age 21	Children and adults
Limitations	Services are subject to the state's definition of *medical necessity:* check state plan for definition of services	Federal: 1. On-site 2. Physician-directed Check state plan for definition of services	Check state plan for definition of services	The group, geographic areas, and services as defined in the state plan	Federal: JCAHO accreditation and certification of need Check state plan for definition of services	Check state plan for definition of services

* If these services are medically necessary to correct a problem or condition identified through an EPSDT screen, the services must be provided to the child even if they are not contained in the state's Medicaid plan.

** Medicaid regulations require Medicaid agencies to assure recipients necessary transportation to and from providers. When a state claims transportation as an administrative expense, the federal match is 50 percent. When the state claims transportation as a service, however, and payment is made to an authorized vendor, it is reimbursed at the state's FMAP rate.

clinic services in their Medicaid plans cover such services as outpatient treatment for adults, children, and youths; partial hospitalization programs operated by community mental health centers; and day treatment programs for children and youths.

Rehabilitative Services. States may also choose to include rehabilitative services within their Medicaid plans. Medicaid law refers to these services as *other diagnostic, screening, preventive, and rehabilitative services.* Like clinic services, rehabilitative services are broadly defined by federal statute. They include:

> any medical or remedial services (provided in a facility, a home, or other setting) recommended by a physician or other licensed practitioner of the healing arts within the scope of their practice under state law, for the maximum reduction of physical or mental disability and restoration of an individual to the best possible functional level.

States have wide latitude under this definition in designing the type of rehabilitative services they wish to offer. Unlike clinic services, rehabilitative services may be medical or remedial, and as a result, are not necessarily driven by a medical model of service delivery. Rehabilitative services may be recommended by a physician or other licensed practitioner of the healing arts, such as a certified social worker, psychologist, or developmental disability specialist, if these professionals are recognized under state law.

Rehabilitative services tend to fall within two major categories: (1) outpatient and day treatment services, and (2) broader psychosocial rehabilitative services. States have used the rehabilitative services option to cover within the Medicaid program such services as psychological testing; individual, group, and family therapy; and therapeutic interventions for children and youths in residential treatment, therapeutic foster care, and group care. Table 11 compares the clinic service option and the rehabilitative services option under Medicaid.

Targeted Case Management. Case management is a separate optional service covered by Medicaid. *Case management* is federally defined as "services that will assist individuals eligible under the [state Medicaid] plan in gaining access to needed medical, social, educational, and other services." Targeted case management differs from other Medicaid services in that it may be delivered solely to certain populations or to certain geographical areas. Targeted case management services do not have to comply with Medicaid's comparability and statewideness requirements.

Targeted case management may be used to meet the case management needs of different groups of individuals. Two groups are specifically mentioned in federal law as possible beneficiaries of case management services: persons with AIDS and persons with chronic mental illness. Table 12 lists some of the states that have used targeted case management for children.

To use the targeted case management option, a state must:

1. Identify the population eligible for case management services.

2. Indicate whether the service will be offered statewide or on a less than statewide basis.

3. Define the components of the case management services.

4. Identify the providers of the service, specifying the qualification requirements.

5. Specify the payment method that will be used to reimburse providers.

A state that seeks to access federal Medicaid funds for case management services should be aware of potential reimbursement issues. A state that offers case management services must not duplicate Medicaid payments under other federal programs for the same service. For child welfare agencies, for example, payments under Medicaid for case management services must not duplicate Title IV-E or Title IV-B payments for the same services. HCFA may require careful documentation. Although the expense of such cost-accounting procedures must be considered, a state's higher federal matching rate for Medicaid (as compared to the 50 percent matching rate for Title IV-E administrative costs, for example) may well offset the administrative costs associated with seeking Medicaid reimbursement.

Inpatient Psychiatric Services to Children through Age 21. The option for inpatient psychiatric services to children through age 21 permits states to cover inpatient therapeutic psychiatric services and room and board costs in qualified facilities for children and youths, unlike the rehabilitative services option, which may be used to finance only the therapeutic services in facilities. This optional service provides an exception to the "institution for mental diseases" (IMD) exclusion that generally bars Medicaid reimbursement for services provided to residents of an IMD.

The IMD exclusion rules are not

Table 11. Clinic Services and Rehabilitative Services under Medicaid

Service Characteristic	Clinic Services	Rehabilitative Services
Type of Service under Medicaid	Optional	Optional
Location of Service	On-site except for services to the homeless	On-site or off-site
Nature of Service	Medical model	Medical or psychosocial model
Physician involvement	Physician must provide or direct services	Physician or other practicioner of the healing arts may recommend and provide services

Table 12. Examples of Case Management Programs for Children

State	Target Population
Alabama	Children with disabilities Children in foster care
Florida	Children with special health care needs Children with mental health problems
Kansas	Ventilator-dependent children
Kentucky	Seriously emotionally disturbed children
Louisiana	Ventilator-dependent children
Maine	Developmentally disabled children ages birth to five
Maryland	Children below age two with HIV High-risk children ages birth to five Infants and toddlers needing early intervention
Michigan	Medically fragile children
Mississippi	High-risk infants and pregnant women
Missouri	High-risk infants (under 1500 grams) and pregnant women
Nebraska	SSI- and AFDC-dependent children with special needs
New Mexico	Developmentally delayed and disabled children Severely emotionally disturbed children
North Carolina	Children with special health care needs
South Carolina	Emotionally disturbed children Children with sickle-cell anemia and children with AIDS
Tennessee	Children ages birth to two
Utah	Children with special health care needs
Virginia	High-risk infants and pregnant women
Washington	All children needing assistance in obtaining services
Wisconsin	Severely emotionally disturbed children

easy to apply. First, a facility is subject to a determination of whether it is an IMD. There is, however, little clear guidance as to the types of organizational structures that constitute "facilities." Likewise, the IMD determination itself is somewhat subjective. HCFA's test for whether a facility is an IMD is the overall character of the institution. HCFA uses one or all of the following criteria in determining whether a facility is an IMD:

1. Is the institution used as an alternative to care in a mental hospital?
2. Is the institution licensed as or holding itself out as a mental institution?
3. Is the institution in proximity to a mental institution?
4. Does the staff specialize in the care of the mentally ill?

If a facility is considered an IMD, the IMD exclusion is then applied on the basis of the size of the facility:

- If the facility has 16 beds or less, the IMD exclusion does not apply. The facility may provide and be reimbursed for services under Medicaid, such as clinic or rehabilitative services, rendered to facility residents.

- If the facility has 17 beds or more and is considered a facility that primarily provides mental health service, the IMD exclusion does apply. The facility may not be reimbursed under Medicaid for services unless the service meets the requirements of the inpatient psychiatric services through age 21 option.

Figure 2 summarizes the questions involved in applying the IMD exclusion rules. For inpatient psychiatric services to children under age 21, federal regulations provide guidance as to who may qualify as providers and the certification of need requirement.

Providers of Inpatient Psychiatric Services. With the amendments to Medicaid law contained in the Omnibus Budget Reconciliation Act of 1990 (OBRA 1990), qualified providers of inpatient psychiatric services to individuals to age 21 now include hospitals or institutions that meet Medicare standards of participation for psychiatric hospitals and other inpatient settings that the Secretary of HHS specifies in regulations.

The OBRA 1990 amendments give HHS the authority to specify the extent to which nonhospital settings may be sites for the provision of inpatient psychiatric services. As of May, 1994, the Secretary of HHS had not yet issued regulations specifying the other inpatient settings that may be reimbursed under Medicaid for inpatient psychiatric services to children and youths. In the past, HCFA has allowed nursing facilities accredited by the Joint Commission on Accreditation of Health Care Organizations (JCAHO) and, in some HCFA regions, JCAHO-accredited residential facilities, to provide such services. The new regulations may change past practice, however, and are likely to address such issues as:

- *The accreditation requirements for providers.* HCFA may rescind its current regulatory requirement of JCAHO accreditation for providers of inpatient psychiatric services to individuals through age 21, particularly in light of the decision by Congress in 1984 to delete any such requirement from Medicaid law itself. In the new regulations, HCFA may give states the authority to determine whether accreditation will be required for the providers of inpatient psychiatric services and, if so, the type of accreditation that will be required.

- *The types of facilities that are eligible for Medicaid reimbursement.* In addition to accreditation issues, the new regulations are likely to specify the types of facilities in addition to hospitals that may provide inpatient psychiatric services to individuals through age 21. Possibilities include nursing facilities and residential treatment centers.

Certification of Need. In order to obtain reimbursement for inpatient psychiatric services, a provider must comply with federal regulations that require a certification that the patient needs the services being provided. A team of physicians and other qualified personnel must certify that the individual requires inpatient care and is expected to improve to a point when inpatient care will no longer be needed. **Transportation.** Transportation services are available under Medicaid both as an option and as a mandated administrative component of services.

Transportation as an Optional Service. A state may choose to cover transportation expenses when an individual needs transportation to receive care that is considered medically necessary. As an optional

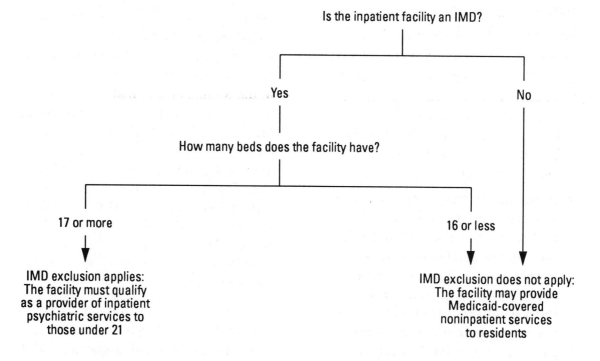

Is the inpatient facility an IMD?

Yes

No

How many beds does the facility have?

17 or more

16 or less

IMD exclusion applies: The facility must qualify as a provider of inpatient psychiatric services to those under 21

IMD exclusion does not apply: The facility may provide Medicaid-covered noninpatient services to residents

Figure 2. The Institutions for Mental Disease (IMD) Exclusion

service, transportation must be furnished by a provider who has qualified as a Medicaid vendor. Federal participation is available to the state at the same federal medical assistance percentage (FMAP) as any other Medicaid service.

Transportation as a Mandatory Administrative Expense. States are required to develop methods, to be included in the state Medicaid plan, to ensure that necessary transportation is available for Medicaid recipients to obtain care. States are free to use a variety of means to meet this requirement, including arrangements with local voluntary organizations or the recipient's friends or family, contracts with transit authorities, and use of state-owned vehicles. Unlike transportation as an optional service, which is reimbursed at the state's FMAP rate, transportation as an administrative cost is matched at a federal financial participation rate (FFP) of 50 percent.

Waiver Programs

Federal law permits states to develop innovative methods of delivering and paying for services under Medicaid through waiver programs. HCFA is authorized to waive certain requirements that Medicaid services must usually meet—such as statewideness, comparability, and freedom of choice, described previously—when states present cost-effective, alternative methods of service delivery or financing. In each instance, a state must design the program in accordance with federal regulations and obtain HCFA approval.

Traditionally, two types of waivers have been sought: home- and community-based waivers and freedom-of-choice waivers.

Home- and Community-Based (HCB) Waivers

HCB waivers permit states to develop home- and community-based programs to help individuals who are institutionalized return to the community and/or to prevent the institutionalization of individuals through the development of community-based supports. HCB waivers permit a state to cover, within a program of home and community services, children or adults who would otherwise be Medicaid eligible only if they were institutionalized. HCB waivers are of two types:

- *Model HCBs.* These waivers may serve a maximum of 200 individuals and may be used to serve only SSI-eligible disabled individuals who would ordinarily lose Medicaid eligibility if they were not being cared for in an institutional setting.

- *Regular HCBs.* These waivers, unlike model HCBs, may serve all individuals up to any target number specified by the state, provided the individuals meet the state-established income and other eligibility criteria. Initial approval of HCB waivers is for three years. Waivers may then be renewed for five-year periods. Regular HCBs have been used by states to provide a range of services to children who would otherwise not be eligible for Medicaid services unless institutionalized.

In comparison with model HCBs, regular HCBs offer a greater range of opportunity for service delivery. ***General Characteristics of HCB Waivers.*** An HCB waiver program allows states to develop a coordinated package of services for a specified or targeted group of individuals who would otherwise be at risk of institutionalization or who are already receiving institutional care and need help to return to the community. Waiver programs provide services to a target population defined by the state and may include, for example, chronically ill children, children with serious emotional disturbances, medically fragile children, or any other population that is defined as likely to require extended care in a hospital, nursing facility, or intermediate care facility for the mentally retarded.

Types of Services. The service package available to waiver participants may include optional Medicaid services that are not made available to other Medicaid beneficiaries under the state plan, as well as services that are not strictly medical in nature. Optional medically-oriented services for the targeted group under an HCB waiver include homemaker and home health care aide in-home services, personal care services, medical day care services, hospice care, and partial hospitalization and clinic services for the chronically mentally ill.

A state also may include certain social services that can assist individuals to remain in the community. Services that may be covered under a HCB waiver and are not otherwise included under Medicaid are:

1. Respite care;

2. Habilitation services that improve the participant's social and adaptive skills;

3. Psychosocial rehabilitation for the mentally ill; and

4. Any other services, other than room and board, requested by the state and approved by the Secretary of HHS, such as the rehabilitation and mental health services component in a residential treatment facility or group care setting.

Many HCB programs also include case management services. These services, however, may now be covered in the state Medicaid plan as an optional service for targeted groups without a waiver. Table 13 gives three examples of HCB waiver programs.

Eligibility. An HCB waiver allows states to provide Medicaid services to persons who would otherwise be ineligible for Medicaid. The state may determine eligibility for waiver participants by using the financial standards that would apply if the beneficiaries were in an institution as opposed to the standards applicable to beneficiaries in the community. The institutional standard may be as high as 300 percent of the state's standard for disability benefits under SSI.

Budget Neutrality. In order to obtain a waiver, the state must show that its project will be *budget neutral*—that the costs associated with its waiver program are no higher than the costs that would have been incurred if the participants had been treated in a nursing home, a hospital, or another institutional setting. The average per capita cost for persons receiving services under the waiver may not exceed the costs that would have been incurred for the same individuals if the waiver had not been granted.

Relationship to EPSDT. Some of the services previously offered through waivers may now be offered through EPSDT, which is a mandatory Medicaid service. Unlike the HCB waiver programs, EPSDT does not require a showing of budget neutrality. Because EPSDT requires that the full range of federal Medicaid-covered services be made available to children and youths in response to the conditions, problems, and illnesses identified through EPSDT screenings (whether or not the services are included in the state's Medicaid plan), EPSDT now provides a way of accessing specialized services that previously might have required a waiver. The HCB waiver, however, permits services to be provided to a broader range of persons than does EPSDT. EPSDT services may

Table 13. Examples of Home- and Community-Based Waivers

State	Population Served	Service Provided
Vermont	Seriously emotionally disturbed children	■ Group residential treatment ■ Specialized foster care for emotionally disturbed and autistic children ■ Intensive home-based services for emotionally disturbed and autistic youths ■ Staffed apartments for older autistic youths
New Mexico	Medically fragile children	■ Case management ■ Homemaker services ■ Personal care ■ In-home respite care ■ Institutional respite care (up to two weeks per year) ■ Physical therapy ■ Occupational therapy ■ Speech therapy ■ Family counseling
Iowa	Persons with AIDS or who are HIV infected	■ Counseling ■ Home health aide services ■ Homemaker services ■ Nursing services ■ Respite services

be provided only to Medicaid-eligible individuals to age 21. HCB waivers may extend eligibility to children, youths, and adults whose income would otherwise render them ineligible for Medicaid.

Questions to Ask Before Seeking an HCB Waiver. To obtain an HCB waiver requires considerable documentation. Thus, it is important to consider whether an HCB waiver is needed to accomplish the goal of the state and whether the necessary documentation is available.

The Goal. A state may wish to use the HCB waiver to expand the services available under its Medicaid program. It is possible, however, that these services may be offered through other avenues without the documentation burdens associated with an HCB waiver. The services may be available through existing Medicaid optional service categories or may be made available through full implementation of EPSDT. Alternatively, a state may wish to broaden the eligibility criteria and bring more persons within Medicaid coverage through a waiver program. Eligibility expansion is generally a sounder basis for seeking an HCB waiver than is service expansion.

Documentation Requirements. In order to obtain HCFA approval, a state must marshal data that (1) establish the costs that would be incurred if the group to be served under the HCB waiver were cared for in institutional settings, and (2) demonstrate that the provision of HCB services will cost Medicaid no more than would the institutional care of the group. The

state must also develop specific criteria to identify individuals who are at risk of institutionalization and who will be served by the HCB waiver.

Freedom-of-Choice Waivers
The term *managed care* is used to describe service delivery systems that coordinate health care through a single point of entry and an enrollment process. Managed care is of growing interest to states as they consider alternative ways of delivering Medicaid services while simultaneously containing costs. Medicaid law permits a variety of managed care arrangements, as reflected in table 14.

If a state wishes to mandate that Medicaid-eligible individuals participate in a managed care program, a freedom-of-choice waiver must be obtained from HCFA.

Two managed care models, both of which require freedom-of-choice waivers, are currently in operation in some states: (1) primary care case management, a managed care option that should not be confused with targeted case management, the optional Medicaid service described previously, and (2) health maintenance organizations (HMOs). Examples of these, respectively, are the Kentucky Patient Access Care (KENPAC) model and CHS/WELL-CORP of Detroit.

Kentucky Patient Access Care (KENPAC): A Primary Care Case Management Model. Like every mandatory service delivery model under Medicaid, KENPAC was approved by HCFA under a freedom-of-choice waiver. The program covers families with children who are Medicaid eligible (approximately 225,000 recipients in 1990). Under the KEN-PAC program, the Medicaid recipient selects or is assigned a physician whose practice functions as the patient's "medical home." Approximately 1,100 physicians—recruited from among general and family practice practitioners, obstetricians and gynecologists, pediatricians, and internists—participate in the program. KENPAC covers 110 of Kentucky's 120 counties.

The primary care physician provides first-line basic medical care on a 24-hour basis. Services include physician visits, pharmacy and laboratory services, hospital inpatient and outpatient services, home health care services, and durable medical equipment. The primary care physician also coordinates access to specialized services. Except for emergency services, referrals for specialized services must be by the written authorization of the physician. Reimbursement to the provider includes both a fee for service and a monthly case management fee of three dollars per enrollee.

Ongoing utilization review monitoring takes place, with data gathered on seven variables: the number of emergency room visits, physician referrals, hospital admissions, laboratory services, pharmacy services, and office visits, and the average cost of service.

Table 14. Managed Care Under Medicaid

Type of Managed Care	Nature of Managed Care	Social Security Act Statutory Authorization
Voluntary participation in health maintenance organizations (HMOs)	Service delivery through HMOs with voluntary participation on the part of Medicaid beneficiaries	Section 1903 (m)
Targeted case management	Case management for specific Medicaid-eligible populations that involves case assessment, coordination, tracking, and monitoring for a defined group under the state Medicaid plan	Optional Service Section 1915 (g)
State plan exceptions for voluntary capitated* programs	Contracted service delivery to individuals in a defined geographic area who choose to utilize the service provider	Section 1915 (a)
Freedom of choice waivers for mandatory enrollment in a managed care plan	Service delivery system in which some or all Medicaid-eligible individuals must participate	Section 1915 (b)

* A capitated program is one in which the health care provider receives a uniform fee, for a fixed period of time, for each individual enrolled under a health care plan.

Cumulative practice patterns are analyzed for each participating physician. In a client survey of its participants, KENPAC found that:

1. Of all participants, 88 percent had selected their own physicians.

2. Of all participants, 79 percent had not changed physicians.

3. Of the pregnant women, 73 percent had received prenatal care during the first trimester.

4. Evaluating satisfaction with their primary care physicians, 67 percent of participants rated their physician above average in accessibility, and 85 percent believed the system succeeded in enhancing doctor-patient relationships.

Studies suggest that approximately $125 million has been saved over the five-year life of the program. Reductions in expenditures are attributed to lower utilization of physician services, decreased use of emergency rooms, and a decrease in the number of inpatient hospital days.

CHS/WELLCORP of Detroit: An Example of HMO Managed Care.

CHS/WELLCORP had its beginning in a Detroit-based health maintenance organization known as Comprehensive Health Services of Detroit, Inc. (CHSD). CHSD began as part of the Model Neighborhood Comprehensive Health Program (MNCHP), designed in 1969 by elected officials of the Detroit Model Neighborhood Agency and health planners from Wayne State University. MNCHP served 10,000 men, women, and children under a contract with the city of Detroit during its first year of operation. In December 1971, MNCHP developed the first HMO-type contract with the Michigan Department of Social Services to provide prepaid health care to Medicaid recipients in its service area.

In 1972, MNCHP formed CHSD to operate as a nonprofit program. By 1975, CHSD's patient population had grown to 20,000, permitting the HMO to reach a financial break-even point and achieve fiscal stability. In 1975, CHSD was issued a Health Maintenance Organization license under the Michigan HMO Act to continue providing HMO services to its members. Actuarial analysis suggested that during its first year in the black, CHSD may have saved the state of Michigan significant dollars in health care costs. In 1979, the HMO became federally qualified, and in 1988, changed its name to Comprehensive Health Services, Inc. (CHS/WELLCORP), its current title.

In 1991, the HMO membership of CHS was approximately 80,000. As a mixed model HMO, CHS/WELLCORP owns and operates three full-service health centers in the Detroit area, serving approximately 47,000 members. Through independent practice associations (IPAs), the corporation also contracts with many physician groups throughout southeast Michigan.

Challenges and Problems in Medicaid Managed Care Systems.

HMO-managed care presents a number of challenges for states seeking to adapt this type of system for Medicaid:

1. Actuarial expertise in setting standard payment methodologies has been difficult to develop.

2. There is still no evaluative data on which to judge the relative benefits of managed care options, including capitation, partial risk, and mandatory and voluntary participation.

3. The process for obtaining freedom-of-choice waivers through HCFA is complex.

4. Medicaid law presents two significant barriers to HMO development: (1) the requirement that not more than 75 percent of the HMO enrollees may be covered by Medicaid or Medicare; and (2) the statutory requirement of "disenrollment without cause," that is, that Medicaid-eligible enrollees must be permitted to disenroll from coverage under the HMO at any time and for any reason.

Recent studies of Medicaid managed care programs have raised a number of questions regarding their impact on access to services. Studies suggest that access to prenatal and children's preventive health care has in many cases been inadequate, and in other cases actually poorer than access to Medicaid fee-for-service physicians.* Several factors have been identified as contributing to inadequate access: (1) the financial disincentives inherent in capitation, (2) the practice of some states under which reimbursement rates for managed care plans are set at 90 to 95 percent of the Medicaid fee-for-service rate, (3) a lack of guidance to providers regarding the nature and scope of "case management," and (4) utilization control procedures that create barriers to care.

Section 1115(a) Waivers

In addition to the two traditional types of waivers, Section 1115(a) waivers are now being sought increasingly by states.

Over the past several years, Section 1115(a) of the Social Security Act has become an important waiver provision in relation to Medicaid. Under Section 1115(a), states may redesign their Medicaid programs in ways that do not comply with the usual federal Medicaid requirements as long as: (1) the redesign is likely to assist in promoting Medicaid program objectives; and (2) the fiscal impact for the federal government is budget neutral.

Since 1982, Arizona has operated its Medicaid program under a Section 1115(a) waiver. Recently, several other states have joined Arizona in obtaining HCFA approval for waiving certain federal Medicaid statutory requirements. In 1993, six states received such approval: Hawaii, Kentucky, Oregon, Rhode Island, South Carolina, and Tennessee. Common to all of

---

* See, for example, Melden, M., "Managed Care: How to Challenge Inadequate Access for Medicaid Beneficiaries." *Clearinghouse Review* 25, 4 (July 1991): 228, citing Goldfarb, Hillman, Eisnberg, Kelley, Cohen, & Dellheim, "Impact of a Mandatory Medicaid Case Management Program on Prenatal Care and Birth Outcomes," *Medical Care* 29 (Jan, 1991); Freund, Rossiter, Fox, Meyer, Hurley, Carey, & Paul, "Evaluation of the Medicaid Competition Demonstrations," *Health Care Financial Review* 11 (Winter 1989); Anderson & Fox, "Lessons Learned from Medicaid Managed Care Approaches," *Health Affairs* 71 (Spring 1987); McCall, Balaban, & Bower, "Evaluation of the Arizona Health Care Cost Containment System," *HCFA Report* No. 500-83-0027 (January 1989).

these waiver projects is expansion of eligibility for Medicaid benefits. Hawaii's program, for example, extends the income eligibility limits for Medicaid to 300 percent of the federal poverty level. Kentucky and Oregon will cover all individuals with incomes up to 100 percent of the federal poverty level.

Five of the six waivers approved in 1993 emphasize managed care. Hawaii, Kentucky, Oregon, Rhode Island, and Tennessee have received approval to restrict participants' freedom of choice of providers. Rhode Island, for example, restricts participants to a single health care plan of their choice for up to one year, and Tennessee requires all participants to receive care through a HMO or preferred provider organization (PPO).

It is anticipated that other states will seek approval for comprehensive Medicaid waiver packages under Section 1115(a)

Summary of Medicaid Services

Multiple service avenues are available through Medicaid to meet the health, mental health, and developmental needs of children and youths. Table 15 presents some of the possibilities that exist within the Medicaid program.

Who are the Medicaid Providers?

Medicaid provider selection and qualification are primarily a state responsibility. Likewise, reimbursement is largely determined by states, although there are some federal requirements regarding efficiency and sufficiency of reimbursement.

Qualifications

In general, states determine the qualification requirements for providers of Medicaid services. One exception is inpatient psychiatric services for individuals through age 21, a service for which there are federal regulatory qualification requirements, including the attainment of JCAHO accreditation.

Reimbursement

States have considerable latitude in determining standards of payment for Medicaid providers. Federal law and regulations do, however, provide guidance.

1. Payment methods and procedures set forth in the state's Medicaid plan must ensure that reimbursement levels are "consistent with efficiency, economy, and quality of care." (42 USC section 1396a [a] [30] [A])

2. Reimbursement rates must be "sufficient to enlist enough providers so that care and services are available under the [state Medicaid] plan at least to the extent that such care and services are available to the general population in the geographic area." (42 USC section 1396a [a] [30] [A])

3. States must report, beginning in April 1990 and each year thereafter, the payment rates for obstetrical and pediatric services to enable the U.S. Department of Health and Human Services to determine whether the rates are adequate to assure equivalent access. HCFA has begun to scrutinize reimbursement rates for obstetrical and pediatric care in several states.

Table 15. Medicaid Services to Meet the Needs of Children and Youths

Need	Mandatory	Optional	Waiver Program
Physical Health			
1. Screening	EPSDT	Clinic Services	
2. Treatment services*	▪ EPSDT ▪ Inpatient hospital services ▪ Outpatient hospital services ▪ Physicians' services ▪ Rural health clinic services	▪ Clinic services ▪ Dental services ▪ Physical therapy ▪ Occupational services ▪ Services for speech, hearing, and language disorders ▪ Prescribed drugs ▪ Prosthetic devices ▪ Eyeglasses ▪ Personal care services ▪ Transportation services ▪ Case management services ▪ Hospice services	Home- and community-based waivers
Mental Health			
1. Screening	EPSDT	Clinic Services	
2. Treatment services*	▪ EPSDT ▪ Inpatient hospital services ▪ Outpatient hospital services	▪ Clinic services ▪ Rehabilitation services ▪ Inpatient psychiatric services through age 21 ▪ Transportation services ▪ Case management services	Home- and community-based waivers
Developmental			
1. Screening	EPSDT	Clinic Services	
2. Treatment services*	▪ EPSDT ▪ Outpatient hospital services	▪ Clinic services ▪ Rehabilitation services	Home- and community-based waivers

* When treatment services are medically necessary to correct, remedy, or modify a condition identified for an EPSDT-eligible child, such services are mandatory for children through age 21.

4. If a state chooses to provide hospice care as a Medicaid service, it must use Medicare reimbursement rates for that care.

Providers may choose not to participate in the Medicaid program, a decision that is frequently linked to reimbursement rates. Providers who choose to participate must accept Medicaid's payment as payment in full for Medicaid-covered services. Low Medicaid fee schedules have become one of the major deterrents to provider participation. As a consequence, some specialties and some geographical areas have very low provider participation rates, making it difficult for Medicaid-eligible individuals to find providers for basic or specialized health care.

Chapter 3
Assessment of the State Medicaid Plan

An assessment of a state's Medicaid plan is important to understanding the Medicaid program in that state. The framework that follows may be used to assess a state's Medicaid plan.

What Groups Are Covered by the State Plan?

I. Medicaid eligibility is mandatory for these groups:

    A. AFDC-eligible individuals.

    B. Children eligible for Title IV-E foster care or adoption assistance.

    C. Pregnant women and their children up to age six, with incomes up to 133 percent of the federal poverty level.

    D. Infants through the age of one year who were born to a Medicaid-eligible mother, as long as the infant remains in the mother's household and the mother is eligible for Medicaid or would be eligible if she were still pregnant.

II. States may select these groups for optional Medicaid coverage:

    A. Pregnant women with family incomes at or below 185 percent of the federal poverty level and their infants up to age one.

    B. Children under non-Title IV-E adoption assistance agreements.

    C. The medically needy. (Note: If the medically needy are covered, ask how the plan defines them.)

    D. Noninstitutionalized disabled children (the Katie Beckett option).

    E. States vary in Medicaid coverage for SSI recipients. (Note: Ask how SSI recipients are treated for Medicaid purposes.)

What Services Are Covered Under the State's Medicaid Plan?

I. EPSDT is a mandatory service and must be in the plan. The following questions permit an assessment of how EPSDT is being implemented in the state.

A. General Questions

1. Who runs the EPSDT program in the state?
2. How are children enrolled in EPSDT?
3. How many Medicaid-eligible children are actually enrolled in EPSDT?
4. How many enrolled children are actually receiving EPSDT services?

B. Screening Questions

1. How do children receive EPSDT screening services?
2. Is there a specific screening protocol that EPSDT screening providers are required to use?
3. Who are the qualified providers of screening services?
4. Are interperiodic screens being provided? If so, how and for what conditions?
5. Are partial screens being provided? If so, what partial screens are provided?

C. Treatment Questions

1. To what extent has the state implemented the expanded treatment requirements of EPSDT?
2. Has the state informed providers and recipients of the expanded coverage for EPSDT diagnostic and treatment services? If so, how?
3. How does the state determine the medical necessity of a requested follow-up diagnostic or treatment service?
4. How are follow-up treatment services provided and reimbursed? Are there screening documentation requirements that must be met before treatment services are reimbursed?

5. Are children receiving specialized treatment for the conditions identified in the screen—especially for mental health and developmental needs?

6. Who is providing medically necessary follow-up treatment?

7. What tracking systems are in place to ensure follow-up?

D. Support Service Questions

1. Is transportation available for EPSDT services?

2. Is assistance provided in scheduling appointments?

II. What optional services are covered under the state's Medicaid plan?

A. Clinic Services

1. Has the state selected the clinic services option?

2. What is the state's definition of clinic services? Consider the state's definition in terms of:
   a) the types of clinic services that may be provided, and by whom;
   b) any medical necessity criteria;
   c) any prior authorization requirements; and
   d) any limits on the amount of service that an individual may receive.

3. Is the definition of clinic services broad enough to cover the specialized mental health and developmental services needed by children?

4. Who are the qualified providers of clinic services? Consider the requirements in light of:
   a) the extent of physician supervision that is required;
   b) the definition of physician supervision; and
   c) the professionals who are qualified to provide services under state law.

B. Rehabilitative Services

1. Does the state cover rehabilitative services?

2. What is the state's definition of rehabilitative services?

3. How broad is the definition?

4. What types of services can be covered under the state's definition?

5. Are there any restrictions on rehabilitative services?

6. Who can provide rehabilitative services?

7. Can the services be authorized and provided by either a physician or another professional?

8. To what extent has the rehabilitative option been used in the state?

9. What flexibility is there to extend the types of service offered under the rehabilitative option to include other services?

C. Targeted Case Management

1. Does the state include case management in the state plan?

2. Who is targeted for case management services? (Note: Consider both geographical areas and specified groups, including children, youths, any specific subgroups, and/or pregnant women.)

3. What range of services is covered under the case management option?

4. Who is eligible to be a provider of case management? Are case managers restricted in terms of providing additional Medicaid services?

5. How do children enter the case management system?

6. Is there any restriction in the individual's freedom of choice to select a provider?

D. Inpatient Psychiatric Care for Individuals through Age 21

1. Does the state cover inpatient psychiatric services for children and adolescents?

2. Who is eligible to provide services?

3. Does the state cover care in residential facilities certified by JCAHO?

4. Is care covered without limits?

5. If limits are imposed, are they related to the median length of stay for children and adolescents in certain types of psychiatric facilities?

6. If limits are low, may they be exceeded in cases of medical or psychological necessity?

7. Is there a requirement that children may be admitted only when alternative community care and treatment cannot meet their needs?

E. Transportation

1. In viewing transportation as an optional Medicaid service, consider:

a) Does the state cover transportation as a service under the plan?

b) If so, how is necessity defined for transportation purposes?

c) Who are the qualified providers of transportation services?

2. In viewing transportation as an administrative expense, consider:

a) What arrangements has the state made to provide necessary transportation as an administrative expense?

b) How are transportation services provided?

III. Does the state plan include any waiver programs?

A. For any home- and community-based services waivers, consider the following:

1. What kind of home- and community-based (HCB) waiver is included in the plan—regular HCB or model HCB?

2. Who is covered under the waiver program?

3. What services are covered?

4. How many people may be served under the waiver?

5. What is the status of the waiver in terms of renewal?

6. If the state does not utilize HCB waivers, what type of HCB waiver might be considered?

7. What purpose would the waiver serve?

   a) Would service expansion be the goal?
   b) Would eligibility expansion be the goal?

8. Can the state provide specific criteria that will permit a valid assessment of imminent risk of institutional care?

9. Can the state show cost-effectiveness and budget neutrality?

B. **For any freedom-of-choice waivers, consider the following:**

   1. What type of program has been approved?

   2. Who is served under the freedom-of-choice waiver?

   3. What geographical areas are served?

C. **For a Section 1115(a) waiver, consider the following:**

   1. What are the major provisions of the waiver?

   2. How has eligibility for Medicaid been modified?

   3. To what extent has freedom of choice been restricted?

   4. What changes have been made in the requirements for Medicaid-certified providers?

Who Is Authorized to Provide Services Under the State's Medicaid Plan?

I. For each service included in the plan, consider the following:

A. Who are the qualified providers for the service?

B. What standards does the state use to determine which providers are qualified to render services?

C. What is the reimbursement structure for the providers of the service?

D. Is there a fee set for the service?

E. Are there total reimbursement caps for public agencies who are providers of services?

F. Is the state using diagnostic-related groups for inpatient care? Is the state using other cost-containment mechanisms for this and other services?

G. How does the Medicaid reimbursement rate compare to the Medicare rate for comparable services?

H. Does the state have flexible rate methods, so that alternative methods can be used to reimburse providers without having to change the state plan?

Section II
Child Welfare and Social Services Funding

Child welfare and other social services may be funded through a variety of sources. There are traditional funding sources for child welfare services under the Social Security Act (Title XX, Title IV-B, and Title IV-E); discretionary grant programs administered by the Administration for Children, Youth and Families (ACYF) of the U.S. Department of Health and Human Services (HHS); and a new program that holds promise for the funding of child welfare services, Title IV-F of the Social Security Act, also known as the JOBS program. The National and Community Service Act may be an additional avenue toward enhanced services for children and youths.

Chapter 4
Traditional Funding Sources for Child Welfare Services

Three federal sources have traditionally funded child welfare services: Title XX, Title IV-B, and Title IV-E of the Social Security Act. The funding mechanisms under each program function somewhat differently, as table 16 illustrates.

The Social Services Block Grant (Title XX): A Summary

Nature of Program
Provides funding to states for a wide range of social services. Services states fund with Title XX dollars include child protective services, foster care, and family preservation activities.
Funding Type
Capped entitlement. No state match required.
For More Information, Contact
Office of Policy, Planning and Legislation, U.S. Department of Health and Human Services, 200 Independence Avenue, SW, Washington, DC 20201. Phone: 202/690–7858.

Title XX: The Social Services Block Grant

The Social Services Block Grant (Title XX), administered by the Administration for Children and Families, U.S. Department of Health and Human Services, gives states broad discretion to provide a wide range of social services. Title XX's objectives are so expansive as to permit virtually every social service activity. The funds are used to:

1. Achieve or maintain economic self-support to prevent, reduce, or eliminate dependency.

2. Achieve or maintain self-sufficiency, including reduction or prevention of dependency.

3. Prevent or remedy neglect, abuse, or exploitation of children and adults unable to protect their own interests, or preserve, rehabilitate, or reunite families.

4. Prevent or reduce inappropriate institutional care by providing for community-based care, home-based care, or other forms of less intensive care.

5. Secure referral or admission for institutional care when other forms of care are not appropriate or provide services to individuals in institutions.

Title XX is a capped entitlement program, funded each year at the amount authorized by Congress. Funds are allocated among the states on the basis of relative population. A state may seek 100 percent reimbursement for services under Title XX up to its allocated amount. Although funding under Title XX is significant, it has eroded seriously over the last decade, with a substantial reduction in Title XX purchasing power.

In FY 1993, $2.8 billion was appropriated for the Title XX Social Services Block Grant. For FY 1994, $3.8 billion was appropriated, reflecting a $1.0 billion increase in the program as a result of the Omnibus Budget Reconciliation Act (OBRA) of 1993 (P.L. 103-66). Those additional funds will be used to assist residents

Table 16. Sources of Funding for Child Welfare Services

Funding Source	Use of Funds	Type of Funding	Federal Share of Costs
Title XX	Social services	Capped entitlement	100%
Title IV-B	Child welfare services	Total amount is appropriated each year	75%
Title IV-E	▪Foster care maintenance (room and board) ▪Adoption assistance payments	Entitlement	▪Foster care maintenance ▪Adoption assistance • Medicaid matching rate for the state: —Administrative costs: 50% —Training: 75% (depending on the type of training

of designated empowerment zones and enterprise communities. Funding will be used to develop and provide services to prevent and treat child abuse and neglect and reunite families, and to provide services to promote economic self-sufficiency. Table 17 provides the state allotments for FY 1995 for the $2.8 billion in Title XX funds that is not designated for empowerment zones and enterprise communities.

Title IV-B

Title IV-B of the Social Security Act provides federal funds for child welfare services under two subparts.

Subpart 1 of Title IV-B

Unlike Title XX, Title IV-B Subpart 1 funds are subject to the Congressional appropriations process, so the amount available each year is not fixed. The statute itself provides for a yearly authorization of $325 million, but Congress has never appropriated funds at that level. In FY 1994, $294.6 million was appropriated for Subpart 1 of Title IV-B.

State public welfare agencies receive Title IV-B funds through two mechanisms. The first $141 million of the amount appropriated under Subpart 1 of Title IV-B is divided equally among the states. Federal law requires that each state have a plan addressing the child welfare services to be provided, training of child welfare staff, administration of the program, and coordination of Title IV-B services with programs funded under Title IV-A (Aid to Families with Dependent Children), Title IV-E (Foster Care and Adoption Assistance), Title XX (the Social Services Block Grant), and state social service programs. Title IV-B child welfare services may include 24-hour emergency caregiver and homemaker services, day care, crisis counseling, emergency shelters,

Child Welfare Services (Title IV-B): A Summary

Nature of Program

Funds child welfare services. Eligible services under Subpart 1 include emergency caretaker and homemaker services, emergency financial assistance, family preservation activities, mental health services, alcohol and drug abuse counseling, and post-adoption services. Eligible services under Subpart 2 include a range of family support and family preservation services.

Funding Type

Subpart 1: Yearly appropriation. 25 percent state match required.

Subpart 2: Capped entitlement, 25 percent state match required.

For More Information, Contact

Administration for Children and Families,

U.S. Department of Health and Human Services , PO Box 1182, Washington, DC 20013. Phone: 202/205–8347.

Table 17. FY 1995 Federal Allotments to States for Title XX Social Service Block Grants

State	Amount	State	Amount
Alabama	45,146,563	Montana	8,994,383
Alaska	6,407,406	Nebraska	17,530,314
American Samoa	104,188	Nevada	14,484,886
Arizona	41,828,247	New Hampshire	12,127,135
Arkansas	26,186,317	New Jersey	85,020,934
California	336,929,151	New Mexico	17,257,427
Colorado	37,876,831	New York	197,778,187
Connecticut	35,813,799	North Carolina	74,694,858
Delaware	7,520,789	Northern Mariana Islands	96,552
District of Columbia	6,429,237	Ohio	120,245,295
Florida	147,228,444	Oklahoma	35,060,629
Georgia	73,690,631		
Guam	482,759	Oregon	32,495,483
Hawaii	12,661,996	Pennsylvania	131,084,400
Idaho	11,646,853	Puerto Rico	14,482,759
Illinois	126,958,336	Rhode Island	10,970,091
Indiana	61,803,637	South Carolina	39,328,595
Iowa	30,694,424	South Dakota	7,760,930
Kansas	27,539,840	Tennessee	54,839,539
Kentucky	40,987,753	Texas	192,724,304
Louisiana	46,794,806	Utah	19,789,826
Maine	13,480,659	Vermont	6,221,843
Maryland	53,573,340	Virgin Islands	482,759
Massachusetts	65,471,249	Virginia	69,608,229
Michigan	103,009,700	Washington	56,062,077
Minnesota	48,901,500	West Virginia	19,778,910
Mississippi	28,533,152	Wisconsin	54,653,975
Missouri	56,684,261	Wyoming	5,097,545
Total			**$2,8000,000,000**

arrangements for access to available emergency financial assistance, temporary child care and respite care to prevent separation of families, home-based family services, services to unmarried parents, provision of and arrangements for mental health or alcohol and drug abuse counseling, and post-adoption services.

The remainder of the appropriated Title IV-B Subpart 1 funds—$155 million in FY 1994 ($294 million minus $141 million)—is available to states that certify that they have in place the additional requirements described in Section 427 of Title IV-B:

1. An inventory of all children in foster care for the six months preceding the inventory, which addresses, for each child, the appropriateness and necessity for placement, whether the child can or should be returned to his or her parents or freed for adoption, and what services are necessary to facilitate return or adoption.
2. A statewide information system.
3. A case review system.
4. A service program to help children return to parents or be placed for adoption.

States certifying compliance with Section 427 are administratively reviewed by the U.S. Department of Health and Human Services. Depending on the degree of the state's compliance with these Section 427 requirements, the state receives additional funding under Title IV-B. Table 18 provides the allotment of Title IV-B Subpart 1 funds for FY 1993 for all states.

Subpart 2 of Title IV-B

The Omnibus Budget Reconciliation Act (OBRA) of 1993 (P.L. 103-66) created a capped entitlement to Title IV-B—Subpart 2. Subpart 2 funds, dedicated to family support and family preservation services, are capped at $895 million over a five-year period. The program requires reauthorization in FY 1998. Funds under Subpart 2 of Title IV-B may be used to create or expand and operate services such as respite care, in-home visiting, drop-in centers, services to improve parenting skills, developmental screening for children, information on and referral to other community services, reunification and preplacement preventive services (such as intensive family preservation), follow-up reunification services, and permanency planning. Foster, adoptive, and biological families are eligible for all services. Table 19 provides the allocations under P.L. 103-66 for each state over the five fiscal years for which the program is authorized.

In addition to the above services, the capped entitlement under Subpart 2 of Title IV-B also will fund grants to state courts to assess and improve procedures, including foster care placement, termination of parental rights, and approval of adoption. Funds may also be used to evaluate state courts' performance and to make recommendations for improvement.

Table 18. FY 1993 Allotment of Funds for Title IV-B Child Welfare Services, Subpart 1

State	Allotment at $294,624,000	Allotment at $141,000,000	State	Allotment at $294,624,000	Allotment at $141,000,000
Alabama	5,798,251	2,771,128	Montana	1,211,809	608,414
Alaska	674,777	355,179	Nebraska	2,136,670	1,044,258
American Samoa	183,371	123,460	Nevada	1,326,362	662,431
Arizona	4,781,390	2,291,632	New Hampshire	1,078,123	545,375
Arkansas	3,495,975	1,685,501	New Jersey	5,307,662	2,539,793
California	30,048,818	14,206,363	New Mexico	2,493,475	1,212,778
Colorado	3,844,876	1,850,024	New York	15,530	7,360,253
Connecticut	2,065,826	1,011,122	North Carolina	8,326,069	3,963,107
Delaware	763,822	397,168	North Dakota	982,955	500,499
District of Columbia	448,212	248,344	Northern Mariana	126,686	96,730
Florida	12,946,006	6,141,615	Ohio	13,052,582	6,191,871
Georgia	8,386,050	3,991,391	Oklahoma	4,428,365	2,125,165
Guam	394,655	223,089	Oregon	3,576,418	1,723,434
Hawaii	1,281,048	641,063	Pennsylvania	12,649,960	6,002,017
Idaho	1,734,494	854,884	Puerto Rico	7,531,906	3,588,624
Illinois	12,157,021	5,769,574	Rhode Island	1,070,439	541,752
Indiana	7,115,189	3,392,123	South Carolina	5,101,221	2,442,447
Iowa	3,565,712	1,718,385	South Dakota	1,107,009	558,996
Kansas	3,083,341	1,490,926	Tennessee	6,328,617	3,021,219
Kentucky	5,192,133	2,485,316	Texas	23,687,998	11,206,947
Louisiana	6,750,330	3,220,076	Utah	3,478,384	1,677,206
Maine	1,533,067	759,902	Vermont	749,584	390,454
Maryland	4,256,288	2,044,023	Virgin Islands	327,662	191,499
Massachusetts	4,566,755	2,190,422	Virginia	6,321,841	3,018,024
Michigan	10,860,253	5,158,089	Washington	5,667,518	2,709,481
Minnesota	5,092,532	2,438,349	West Virginia	2,564,554	1,246,294
Mississippi	4,437,556	2,129,499	Wisconsin	6,033,052	2,881,847
Missouri	6,217,709	2,968,921	Wyoming	751,264	391,247
Total				**$292,624,000**	**$141,000,000**

Title IV-E: Foster Care Maintenance and Adoption Assistance

Unlike Title IV-B, Title IV-E is an entitlement program that funds foster care maintenance (or room and board costs), for eligible children, and adoption assistance payments for children with special needs. Children are Title IV-E eligible and, therefore, entitled to federal financial participation in the costs of their foster care placement, if they enter foster care from families who are eligible for Aid to Families with Dependent Children (AFDC) or from families who would have been AFDC eligible if the family had applied for AFDC benefits. Children with special needs are eligible for adoption assistance payments if they were eligible for Title IV-E at the time of their foster care placement or became eligible for SSI before adoption. In FY 1994, Congress allocated $2.6 billion for foster care maintenance payments and $317.40 million for adoption assistance.

The Title IV-E Plan

Each state must have a Title IV-E plan that is written, reviewed, and approved by the state governor and the regional office for the Administration for Children and Families of the U.S. Department of Health and Human Services. It must include:

1. A case review system.
2. A case plan for each child that
   - is a written and discrete part of the case record;
   - is developed within a reasonable period of time, no later than 60 days from the date the state assumes responsibility for providing services to the child;
   - discusses how to achieve placement in the least restrictive, most family-like setting, and in close proximity to parent's home; and
   - describes the services to prevent family separation or to reunify the child and family.
3. Dispositional hearings within 18 months of the date of the original foster care placement.

Foster Care Maintenance and Adoption Assistance (Title IV-E): A Summary

Nature of Program

Provides funding to states for foster care maintenance, adoption assistance, payments for children with special needs, and assistance to youths moving from foster care into independent living.

Funding Type:

Entitlement. Level of state match varies.

For More Information, Contact

Children's Bureau, Administration for Children and Families,
U.S. Department of Health and Human Services, PO Box 1182, Washington, DC 20013.
Phone: 202/205–8347.

Table 19. Distribution of Funds under P.L. 103–66 (Title IV-B, Subpart 2)

State	FY 1994*	FY 1995**	FY 1996**	FY 1997**	FY 1998**
Alabama	$1,199,639	$2,880,911	$4,334,445	$4,646,141	$4,957,838
Alaska	77,754	186,726	280,936	301,139	321,341
American Samoa	90,857	122,095	149,102	154,893	160,684
Arizona	1,005,253	2,414,096	3,632,104	3,893,294	4,154,484
Arkansas	577,604	1,387,105	2,086,955	2,237,031	2,387,107
California	6,925,694	16,631,924	25,023,389	26,822,863	28,622,330
Colorado	616,481	1,480,468	2,227,423	2,387,600	2,547,778
Connecticut	444,311	1,067,004	1,605,350	1,720,793	1,836,236
Delaware	105,524	253,413	381,271	408,688	436,106
District of Columbia	194,386	466,814	702,341	752,847	803,353
Florida	2,615,879	6,281,986	9,451,497	10,131,169	10,810,840
Georgia	1,555,088	3,734,514	5,618,724	6,022,775	6,426,826
Guam	129,726	219,181	296,518	313,102	329,687
Hawaii	194,386	466,814	702,341	752,847	803,353
Idaho	155,509	373,451	561,872	602,278	642,683
Illinois	2,504,802	6,015,235	9,050,160	9,700,970	10,351,781
Indiana	938,606	2,254,046	3,391,302	3,635,175	3,879,049
Iowa	427,649	1,026,991	1,545,149	1,656,263	1,767,377
Kansas	372,110	893,616	1,344,481	1,441,164	1,537,848
Kentucky	1,083,007	2,600,822	3,913,040	4,194,433	4,475,826
Louisiana	1,888,321	4,534,767	6,822,737	7,313,370	7,804,003
Maine	244,371	586,852	882,942	946,436	1,009,930
Maryland	760,882	1,827,244	2,749,162	2,946,858	3,144,554
Massachusetts	960,822	2,307,396	3,471,569	3,721,215	3,970,861
Michigan	2,304,862	5,535,083	8,327,752	8,926,614	9,525,475
Minnesota	655,358	1,573,831	2,367,891	2,538,170	2,708,448
Mississippi	1,155,208	2,774,210	4,173,910	4,474,062	4,774,214
Missouri	1,149,654	2,760,873	4,153,843	4,452,552	4,751,261
Montana	133,293	320,101	481,605	516,238	550,871
Nebraska	233,263	560,177	842,809	903,416	964,024
Nevada	161,063	386,789	581,939	623,787	665,636
New Hampshire	94,416	226,738	341,137	365,669	390,200
New Jersey	1,132,992	2,720,860	4,093,642	4,388,022	4,682,402
New Mexico	455,419	1,093,679	1,645,484	1,763,813	1,882,142
New York	4,043,228	9,709,736	14,608,684	15,659,216	16,709,749
North Carolina	1,160,762	2,787,548	4,193,976	4,495,572	4,797,167

Table 19 (continued). Distribution of Funds under P.L. 103–66 (Title IV-B, Subpart 2)

State	FY 1994*	FY 1995**	FY 1996**	FY 1997**	FY 1998**
North Dakota	99,970	240,076	361,204	387,178	413,153
Northern Mariana	80,428	96,047	109,551	112,446	115,342
Ohio	2,782,496	6,682,112	10,053,503	10,776,466	11,499,429
Oklahoma	694,296	1,667,194	2,508,359	2,688,739	2,869,119
Oregon	510,957	1,227,055	1,846,152	1,978,912	2,111,672
Pennsylvania	2,360,401	5,668,459	8,528,421	9,141,713	9,755,004
Puerto Rico	1,442,746	3,498,785	5,276,321	5,657,497	6,038,672
Rhode Island	188,832	453,477	682,274	731,337	780,400
South Carolina	805,313	1,933,945	2,909,697	3,118,937	3,328,178
South Dakota	127,739	306,764	461,538	494,728	527,918
Tennessee	1,327,378	3,187,674	4,795,983	5,140,869	5,485,755
Texas	5,376,160	12,910,748	19,424,733	20,821,595	22,218,457
Utah	294,356	706,890	1,063,544	1,140,025	1,216,506
Vermont	105,524	253,413	381,271	408,688	436,106
Virgin Islands	117,401	188,397	249,776	262,938	276,101
Virginia	927,499	2,227,371	3,351,168	3,592,155	3,833,143
Washington	938,606	2,254,046	3,391,302	3,635,175	3,879,049
West Virginia	572,050	1,373,768	2,066,888	2,215,521	2,364,154
Wisconsin	821,975	1,973,957	2,969,897	3,183,467	3,397,037
Wyoming	77,754	186,726	280,936	301,139	321,341
Total State Grants	$57,400,000	$137,500,000	$206,750,000	$221,600,000	$236,450,000
Indian Set-aside	$600,000	$1,500,000	$2,250,000	$ 2,400,000	$2,550,000
Set-aside for Training, Technical Assistance, and Evaluation	$2,000,000	$6,000,000	$6,000,000	$6,000,000	$6,000,000
Amount for Courts	0	$5,000,000	$10,000,000	$10,000,000	$10,000,000
Subtotal	$2,600,000	$12,500,000	$18,250,000	$18,400,000	$18,550,000
Total Appropriation	$60,000,000	$150,000,000	$225,000,000	$240,000,000	$255,000,000

 * FY 1994: State allotments are based on the statutory formula using Food Stamp data (section 433(c)).
   Allotments for the territories and insular areas are based on the title IV-B formula (section 433(b)).
   The table also includes the set-asides fot grants to Indian Tribes and Statecourts, and grants for research, evaluation, and training and technical assistance (section 430(d)).

** FY 1995-98: State allotments for these years should be used only for planning purposes. They are based on current information and will need to be revised when future Food Stamp data and appropriations are known.

4. Periodic reviews of foster care maintenance and adoption assistance payments and licensing and approval standards for child care institutions and family foster homes.

5. Safeguards to restrict use and disclosure of information.

6. A designated authority that establishes and maintains standards for foster family homes and child care institutions.

7. In each case, the use of reasonable efforts prior to placement to prevent or eliminate the need to separate the family and to make it possible for the child to return home.

Title IV-E Components

Title IV-E funding falls into five categories: foster care maintenance, adoption assistance, training, child placement and administrative costs, and transitional independent living services. Table 20 summarizes the components of Title IV-E.

Table 20. Title IV-E

Title IV-E Component	What the Funds Cover	Federal Share of Costs
Foster care maintenance	Foster care room and board; no services	The state's Medicaid match rate
Adoption assistance	Cash payments for children with special needs; no services	The state's Medicaid match rate
Training	Training for child welfare staff from the public and private sector, foster parents, and adoptive parents	75% of the training costs as allocated to the Title IV-E eligible children in the state's caseload*
Child placement and administrative costs	▪ Case plan management ▪ Pre-placement services ▪ Eligibility determination ▪ Administrative overhead	50% of costs as allocated to the Title IV-E eligible children in the state's caseload*
Transitional independent living	Independent living services beginning at age 16 for all youths in out-of-home care (not limited to Title IV-E eligible youth); services may continue up to six months from discharge from foster care	Not applicable; this program receives an appropriation each year. In FY 1994, $70 million was appropriated.

*Training and child placement and administration costs first must be allocated to the proportion of children in out-of-home care who are Title IV-E eligible. For example, if the state spent $1 million for child welfare training and 50 percent of the children in foster care were Title IV-E eligible, the federal government would pay 75 percent of $500,000 (50 percent of $1 million) for a total federal payment of $375,000. Similarly, child placement and administrative costs, reimbursed at a 50 percent rate, must be allocated according to the Title IV-E eligibility rate.

Foster Care Maintenance. Title IV-E foster care maintenance payments are available for eligible children in eligible facilities. Children are eligible for Title IV-E when (1) they are AFDC eligible and (2) there is a judicial determination that they require out-of-home care or there is a voluntary placement agreement. Eligible facilities must be licensed or certified by the state and, if a public institution, have fewer than 25 beds. Rate structures under Title IV-E are based on state-established payment schedules and are enhanced in many states with add-ins for special needs and one-time expenses. For group homes and residential centers, rates are usually provider-specific, based on historic costs and services provided.

Adoption Assistance Payments. Adoption assistance payments are available to eligible children with special needs through age 18 (or at state option to age 21 if the child has physical or mental disabilities). Special needs are broadly defined under federal law. States determine special needs on the basis of such criteria as ethnic minority membership, age (older children and adolescents), medical impairment, physical disability, mental disability or retardation, and emotional disturbance or maladjustment. Eligibility is tied to AFDC eligibility or SSI eligibility. In some states, children who are not eligible under Title IV-E may participate in state subsidized adoption programs.

Training. Any amount may be spent by a state on training under Title IV-E, but all training activities and costs must be included in the state's training plan under Title IV-B. The training may be directed to any child welfare issue or any skill needed by child welfare staff. Staff executives, on-line workers and supervisors, and foster and adoptive parents in both the public and private sectors may be trained. Recoverable training costs include the costs associated with the trainer or training unit, including salaries, the costs of providing training, and the costs of going to training. The federal participation rate is 75 percent of the costs attributable to the Title IV-E eligible children in the state's foster care and adoption assistance caseloads.

Child Placement and Administrative Costs. The extent of federal participation in Title IV-E child placement and administrative costs is determined on the basis of allowable costs, allowable time, and the percentage of children in the state's foster care and adoption assistance caseloads who are Title IV-E eligible.

Allowable costs are determined by the state with regional HHS approval. Allowable costs include: case plan development, preplacement services, preparation for court, referral for services, placement services, case review, case management, recruitment and licensing of foster homes and institutions, rate setting, and eligibility determination. Allowable time can be determined through a variety of mechanisms, including random moment sampling. Noncovered time includes time spent in fundraising, counseling, education, and medical services. Allowable costs and allowable time, once determined, must by multiplied by the percentage of children who are

Title IV-E eligible. The result of this calculation determines the federal financial participation that a state receives.

The Independent Living Program (ILP). Unlike other Title IV-E components, ILP is not tied to Title IV-E eligibility. It provides states with funding for services targeted to youths 16 years and older who are making the transition from out-of-home care to independent living, irrespective of the youth's Title IV-E eligibility. Services may be continued for up to six months after youths leave care. The Omnibus Budget Reconciliation Act of 1993 (P.L. 103-66) permanently authorized the Independent Living Program at its current funding level of $70 million yearly.

Chapter 5
Additional Sources
of Child Welfare
Funding

In addition to the traditional sources of funding for child welfare services, there are other funding sources that may be utilized: discretionary funds, administered by the Administration for Children, Youth and Families of the U.S. Department of Health and Human Services, for programs related to child welfare services; Title IV-F of the Social Security Act (the JOBS program), administered by the Administration for Children and Families; and the National and Community Service Trust Act, administered by the Corporation on National and Community Service.

Discretionary Funds— The Administration for Children, Youth and Families: A Summary

Nature of Program
Provides funding for a broad range of child welfare programs, including child protective services, foster care, family preservation, and reunification and adoption.
Funding Type
Determined annually by the U.S. Department of Health and Human Services.
For More Information
Children's Bureau, Administration for Children and Families, PO Box 1182, Washington, DC 20013.
Phone: 202/205–8347.

Discretionary Funds

The Administration for Children, Youth and Families (ACYF) of the U.S. Department of Health and Human Services administers a number of discretionary grant programs that fund services for the children, youths, and families served by the child welfare and social service system. Funded on a competitive basis, these programs address a wide range of issues: substance abuse, HIV infection and AIDS, adoption, housing and services for homeless youths, and research. Table 21 summarizes some of the major features of selected ACYF discretionary grant programs.

Title IV-F of the Social Security Act

A federal program that increasingly is being considered as a possible source of funding for child welfare services is Title IV-F of the Social Security Act, also known as The Family Support Act of 1988 and as the Job Opportunities and Basic Skills Training Program (JOBS). This program is administered by the Administration for Children and Families, U.S. Department of Health and Human Services.

Each state is required to establish and operate a program under JOBS, which replaced the Work Incentive (WIN) program as of October 1, 1990. JOBS is designed to assure that needy families with children obtain the education, training, and employment they need to become self-sufficient. The Title IV-F program reaches AFDC families with children—families with whom child welfare and other social service agencies traditionally work—and provides funding for supportive services as well as job training.

Funding

JOBS program funding is a capped entitlement. Funding was capped at $1 billion for each of the fiscal years 1991 through 1993, then at $1.1 billion for FY 1994, $1.3 billion for FY 1995, and $1 billion for each year thereafter.

Job Opportunities and Basic Skills Training (JOBS)— Title IV-F: A Summary

Nature of Program

Funds states to provide job training, education, and employment-related services to AFDC-eligible families with children. Supportive services related to employability are covered activities.

Funding Type

Capped entitlement. State match varies depending on the activity.

For More Information

Office of Family Assistance, Administration for Children and Families, U.S. Department of Health and Human Services, Aerospace Building—5th Floor, 370 L'Enfant Promenade, SW, Washington, DC 20447. Phone: 202/401–9275.

Table 21. Discretionary Child Welfare Grant Programs

Program	Type of Service	Eligible Entities	Appropriations (in millions of dollars)	
			FY 93	FY 94
Abandoned Infants Assistance Act	Services for children who are abandoned or at risk of abandonment because of HIV infection or drug exposure; training programs for service providers; resource coordination programs	Public and nonprofit private entities	$13.6	$14.6
Emergency Child Protection Grant	Services for children and families who require child welfare services because of substance abuse in the family	Community and mental health agencies; nonprofit youth-serving organizations with experience in providing child abuse prevention services	$19.2	$19.0
Child Welfare Research and Demonstration	Research and demonstration activities in the field of child welfare, specifically in the areas of prevention and specialized services related to foster care, reunification, and adoption	States, local governments, and nonprofit institutions, agencies, and organizations	$6.5	$6.5
Transitional Living for Homeless Youth	Housing and independent living services for youths who are homeless	Public and private nonprofit agencies with experience in serving youths who are homeless or in need of independent living services	$11.8	$12.2
Increased Adoptive Placements of Minority Children	Services to enhance timely adoptive placements for children of color	Public or private nonprofit licensed child welfare, adoption agencies, incorporated adoptive family groups, and community-based organizations	$2.5	Not available
Postlegal Adoption Services	Services to adopted children and adoptive parent	Public or nonprofit licensed child welfare adoption agencies and incorporated adoptive-parent groups	$2.5	Not available

The federal matching rate is 90 percent of expenditures up to the amount allotted to the state under the WIN program in FY 1987 (a total of $126 million for all states). For funds in excess of the 1987 WIN allocation, the federal share of program expenditures is set at the state's Medicaid matching rate, with a minimum federal match of 60 percent for nonadministrative costs and personnel costs for full-time staff working on the JOBS program. The federal match for other administrative costs is 50 percent.

Federal law requires that the federal match be reduced to 50 percent on all program components unless 55 percent of the state's funds are spent on the following groups:

1. Families in which the custodial parent is under age 24 and (a) has not completed high school, (b) is not enrolled in a high school or an equivalent course, or (c) has little or no work experience in the preceding year.

2. Families in which the youngest child is within two years of being ineligible for assistance because of age.

3. Families that have received assistance for more than 36 months during the preceding 60-month period.

Table 22 summarizes the federal matching percentages for each component of the JOBS program.

Services and Activities

The state welfare agency responsible for the administration of the AFDC program receives and administers JOBS funds. Each state, through the administering agency, is required to provide a broad range of services and activities under JOBS, including the following:

1. Educational activities, as appropriate for each participant, including high school or equivalent education combined with training, basic and remedial education to achieve a basic literacy level, and education

Table 22. The Title IV-F JOBS Program: Federal Financial Participation (FFP)

JOBS Activity	FFP Rate
■ Cost of services up to amount allocated to state under 1987 WIN formula level	90%*
■ Cost of services above amount allocated to state under 1987 WIN formula level	State's Medicaid match rate, minimum of 60%
■ Nonadministrative costs, including personnel costs for full-time staff for JOBS program	60%*
■ Other administrative costs	50%

*Subject to a reduction to 50% if 55% of funds are not spent on high-priority groups

for individuals with limited English proficiency.

2. Jobs skills training.

3. Job readiness activities to help prepare participants for work.

4. Job development and job placement.

At least two of the following services also must be provided:

1. Group and individual job search.

2. On-the-job training.

3. Work supplementation programs.

4. Community work experience programs.

Exempt Recipients

Certain individuals who receive AFDC benefits are exempt from participating in the JOBS program. Exempt recipients include (a) persons who are ill, incapacitated, or of advanced age; (b) persons needed in the home because of the illness or incapacity of another member of the household; (c) parents caring for a young child, under age three or a younger age selected by the state (but not younger than age one); (d) persons employed 30 or more hours a week; (e) children under age 16 and attending an elementary, secondary, or vocational school full-time; and (f) women in at least the second trimester of pregnancy and residing in an area where the program is not available. Recipients of AFDC benefits who are exempt may participate in the program on a voluntary basis.

The Employability Plan

As part of the JOBS program, the JOBS staff assesses and reviews the needs and skills of participants and, on that basis, develops individual employability plans. The assessment and review must address three areas:

1. The needs of the participant, including educational needs; child care needs; skills, prior work experience, and employability; and, perhaps most importantly for social service providers, the participant's supportive service needs.

2. The family circumstances.

3. The needs of any child of any participant.

Based on the assessment, an employability plan must be developed that:

1. Sets forth the employment goal;

2. Explains the services to be provided by the state, the available program resources, local employment opportunities and steps to be taken by the participant;

3. Includes information on child care and, on request, assistance in obtaining child care; and

4. Identifies and addresses the participant's supportive services needs.

Supportive Services

The supportive service needs of a JOBS participant can be identified and addressed through collaboration between the AFDC and child welfare staff working with the participant and her/his family. Supportive service needs must be tied to employability. They may include such services as in-home intensive counseling, substance abuse treatment, case management, therapeutic intervention services for a participant's child, and other services traditionally provided by child welfare professionals, all of which can be linked to the participant's ultimate employability. Through inclusion of such supportive services in the individual's employability plan, Title IV-F funds become available to finance the services necessary to meet those needs.

Participation Rates/Work Requirements

Certain minimum participation standards are established for FY 1990 to FY 1995. In FY 1990 and FY 1991, at least 7 percent of the individuals in the AFDC caseload who were required to participate in the JOBS program had to be enrolled. The minimum participation rates for subsequent fiscal years are 11 percent for FY 1992 to FY 1993, 15 percent for FY 1994, and 20 percent for FY 1995.

A parent in the AFDC-Unemployed Parent (AFDC-UP) program under Title IV-A must participate at least 16 hours per week in work activity or, in certain cases, in educational activity. Beginning in 1994, states must achieve the following percentages for AFDC-UP families in the JOBS program: 40 percent for FY 1994; 50 percent for FY 1995; 60 percent for FY 1996; and 75 percent for FY 1997 and FY 1998.

In assigning participants to any program activity, the state agency must assure that:

1. Each assignment takes into account the physical capacity, skills, experience, health and safety, family responsibilities, and place of residence of the participant.

2. No participant is required, without his or her consent, to travel an unreasonable distance from his or her home or remain away from such home overnight.

3. Individuals are not discriminated against on the basis of race, sex, national origin, religion, age, or disabling condition.

4. The conditions of participation are reasonable, taking into account in each case the proficiency of the participant and the child care and other supportive services needs of the participant.

5. Each assignment is based on available resources, the participant's circumstances, and local employment opportunities.

Transitional Medical Assistance

States must extend Medicaid coverage for one year to families who leave the AFDC cash assistance program because of increased earnings or who lose the earnings disregards for the AFDC program. During the second six months of the one-year time period, states may impose an income-related premium on families with earnings (less necessary child care expenses) above the federal poverty level.

The National and Community Service Trust Act

The National and Community Service Trust Act, signed into law on September 21, 1993, is designed to mobilize individuals, including young people in out-of-home care, to serve their communities and counties. The centerpiece of the effort is a new program to offer educational awards to individuals who make a substantial commitment to service. In addition, the law:

- Extends programs in the National and Community Service Act of 1990 that enhance elementary and secondary education through community service in schools, support after-school and summer programs for school-age youths, and fund service programs on college campuses.

- Supports a Civilian Community Corps to provide service opportunities in areas adversely affected by defense cutbacks.

- Supports the Points of Light Foundation to enhance volunteerism.

- Extends the Volunteers in Service to America (VISTA) program, and the Older American Volunteer program.

The focus of national and community service is to address unmet educational, environmental, human, and public safety needs. A National Service Corporation and State Commissions establish priorities among the needs that the programs must address.

Authorizations for national and community service programs are $300 million for FY 1994; $500 million for FY 1995; and $700 million for FY 1996. The total appropriation for FY 1994 for all national and community service activities is $370 million.

The Educational Award Program
Under the National and Community Service Trust Act's Educational Awards program, individuals may complete their service before, during, or after post-secondary education. Participants must be age 17 or older (civilian community corps participants may be age 16 or older) and high school graduates or, in most cases, agree to achieve their GED.

To earn an education award, a participant in a designated program may serve a term of service full-time over one year or part-time over two years (three years in the case of students). The term of service is 1,700 hours for full-time service and 900 hours for part-time service (with a correspondingly smaller award). An individual may serve up to two terms and earn up to two educational awards.

The National and Community Service Trust Act Program: A Summary

Nature of Program
Funds a variety of activities to enhance national and community service by individuals, including youths in out-of-home care.
Funding Type
Amount is appropriated each year.
For More Information
The Corporation for National and Community Services, 1100 Vermont Avenue, NW, Washington, DC 20525. Phone: 202/606–5000.

Educational awards of $4,725 will be provided for full-time service. These awards may be used to repay loans for higher education or to pay for higher education or training. They will be federally funded and deposited into a national service trust on behalf of all participants accepted into the program.

Any program stipends provided must meet certain guidelines. Programs may provide stipends that are no less than the amount received by VISTA volunteers and no greater than twice that amount. Federal support will be limited to a match of 85 percent of the VISTA allowance, with programs paying any stipend costs above that amount.

All participants without access to health insurance will receive health care coverage. Federal dollars will pay up to 85 percent of the cost of these benefits. Participants will receive child care assistance if needed.

Serve-America

A number of Serve-America programs have been reauthorized, expanded, or modified under the National and Community Service Trust Act:

- The Service Learning Program is designed to build a foundation for service among young people. Programs may be partnerships of local educational agencies and community based organizations.
- The School-Age Youth Community-Based Program provides grants for community-based organizations for programs to involve school-age youth in community service.
- The Higher Education Innovative Projects may be designed by higher education institutions, consortia of such institutions, or partnerships of higher education institutions and nonprofit institutions for student community service programs or programs to train teachers in service learning methods.

National and Community Service and Child Welfare and Social Services

The linkages between national and community service and child welfare and social services are important at two levels. First, young people being served through the child welfare and social services systems are potential participants in national and community service programs. Second, agencies and programs that provide child welfare and social services may serve as sites for national and community services activities, benefitting from the efforts of young people who have chosen to serve.

Section III
Income Support
Services

Four major sources of federal funding address the income needs of children and families: the Supplemental Security Income (SSI) program (Title XVI); the Aid to Families with Dependent Children (AFDC) program (Title IV-A); the Title IV-A Emergency Assistance program; and the Child Support Program (Title IV-D). All four programs are authorized by the Social Security Act.

Chapter 6
Supplemental Security Income (SSI)

Supplemental Security Income (SSI): A Summary

Nature of Program
Provides monthly cash benefits to blind and disabled children, youths, and adults and to the aged who meet financial eligibility criteria. In most states, the federal benefit is supplemented by a state payment. Maximum federal benefit: $446 per month in 1994. The definition of disability has broadened under recent changes in the law, and as a result, more low-income children with disabilities are likely to qualify for SSI benefits.

Funding Type
Federal entitlement.

For More Information
Office of Public Inquiries, Annex Room 4100, Social Security Administration, U.S. Department of Health and Human Services, Baltimore, MD 21235.
Phone: 410/965–2736.

The Supplemental Security Income (SSI) program, administered by the Social Security Administration, provides monthly cash benefits to aged, blind, or disabled individuals who meet financial eligibility criteria. A disabled child who is eligible may receive a federal cash benefit of up to $446 a month in 1994, up from $434 in

1993. The exact amount of the benefit depends on family income. In most states, the federal cash benefit is enhanced by a state supplemental benefit. In addition, in most states, SSI eligibility carries with it automatic eligibility for Medicaid. In order to qualify for SSI, a child must be financially eligible and either blind or disabled.

Financial Eligibility

A child's financial eligibility for SSI is based on an assessment of the income and resources available to the child. Income and resources include those attributed directly to the child as well as those attributed to his or his parents. Under a process called *deeming*, the Social Security Administration (SSA) takes parental income and resources into account in making the determination of financial eligibility for a child. SSA, however, permits certain deductions and exclusions under its parental deeming rules, which tend to be more liberal than the deeming rules that apply when spousal income is considered for a blind or disabled adult. As a result, a parent's income may be higher than that allocated a spouse for purposes of determining financial eligibility for SSI.

The income and resource deeming rules that relate to financial eligibility for SSI tend to be quite complicated. Consequently, advocates and service providers should not make assumptions about a child's financial eligibility. *All children who may be eligible should be referred to SSA for a determination of financial eligibility.* In general, financial eligibility is determined by SSA on the basis of income and resources.

Income

For SSI purposes, income is divided into two categories: earned income and unearned income. SSI financial eligibility criteria allow for higher levels of earned income than for unearned income.

Earned Income. Earned income counted in determining SSI eligibility is primarily salary and wages. Certain earned income is not counted by SSA: earned income credit (EIC) payments; up to $400 a month (under a yearly limit of $1620) earned by an unmarried child who is disabled, under age 18, and a student; and money used to pay certain work expenses for individuals who are blind or disabled.

Unearned Income. Unearned income includes such items as interest payments and dividends. Many government benefits are not counted by SSA as unearned income: food stamps, benefits under the Special Supplemental Food Program for Women, Infants, and Children (WIC), housing and home energy assistance payments, foster care payments for a child who is not applying for SSI, one-third of the child support payments made by an absent parent, and grants or loans for education.

Resources

Certain assets are considered resources and are subject to valuation for SSI financial eligibility purposes: cash, bank accounts, bonuses, cars, boats, and personal belongings. Other assets are not counted as resources: the family home and the land on which it is located, personal belongings and household goods up to $2,000, a car needed for work or to obtain medical care, a life insurance policy with a value up to $1,500, an IRA or other employment-based pension plan, and property needed for work, such as equipment or farmland.

Blindness or Disability

A child must first be determined to be financially eligible for SSI before SSA will consider whether the child meets the eligibility requirements related to blindness or disability.

Blindness

Under SSA criteria, an individual is blind if his or her vision cannot be corrected to better than 20/200 in the better eye or if the visual field is 20 degrees or less, even with corrective lenses.

Disability

Under SSA criteria, a child is considered disabled if the child's physical or mental impairment is as severe as a condition that would prevent an adult from working and the condition is expected to last at least 12 months or to result in the child's death. The procedures used for determination of childhood disabilities have undergone significant changes over the last few years, largely as a result of the U.S. Supreme Court's 1990 decision in *Zebley v. Sullivan*. Additionally, SSA has significantly expanded the criteria under which children may qualify for SSA benefits as a result of mental disability. These changes mean that children with disabilities are now more likely to qualify for SSI benefits.

In *Zebley v. Sullivan*, the U.S. Supreme Court invalidated prior practices of SSA regarding the determination of disability in children. Prior to the Court's *Zebley* ruling, SSA had used a two-step process in evaluating adult disability, but a "listings only" approach for children. For adults, SSA initially determined whether an applicant had a condition that was on one of the agency's "Listings of Impairments"—disabling conditions for which SSI eligibility might be established. If the condition was not listed, SSA then considered whether the adult had a condition that "equaled" a condition on the listing. If the adult's condition was neither listed nor equal to a listed condition, SSA then allowed a second step—a functional assessment to determine if the adult was nevertheless unable to work.

For children, however, SSA employed only the listings approach, and did not undertake a functional assessment if the child's condition was not listed or equal to a listed condition. The Court held that SSA's "listings only" approach for children was improper, and ordered SSA to develop new rules that would require an individual assessment of each child's functional limits and disability. Under the *Zebley* decision, children must now be accorded the same assessment process as adults—an initial determination followed by a functional assessment to determine whether the child's impairment keeps her or him from doing everyday things most children of the same age do. If the functional assessment results in such a determination, the child is considered disabled and entitled to SSI benefits. Figure 3 illustrates the sequential process that SSA must now

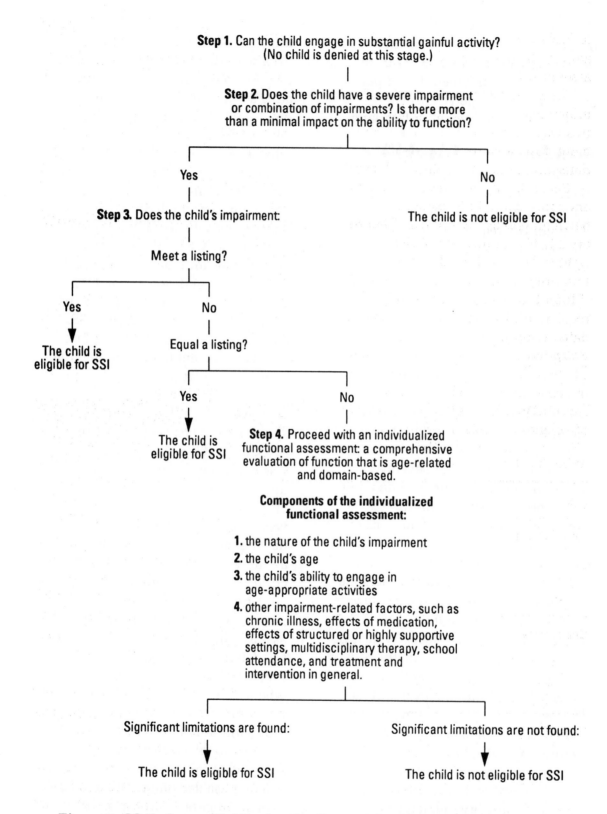

Step 1. Can the child engage in substantial gainful activity?
(No child is denied at this stage.)

Step 2. Does the child have a severe impairment
or combination of impairments? Is there more
than a minimal impact on the ability to function?

Yes

No

Step 3. Does the child's impairment:

The child is not eligible for SSI

Meet a listing?

Yes

No

The child is
eligible for SSI

Equal a listing?

Yes

No

The child is
eligible for SSI

Step 4. Proceed with an individualized
functional assessment: a comprehensive
evaluation of function that is age-related
and domain-based.

**Components of the individualized
functional assessment:**

1. the nature of the child's impairment

2. the child's age

3. the child's ability to engage in
age-appropriate activities

4. other impairment-related factors, such as
chronic illness, effects of medication,
effects of structured or highly supportive
settings, multidisciplinary therapy, school
attendance, and treatment and
intervention in general.

Significant limitations are found:

Significant limitations are not found:

The child is eligible for SSI

The child is not eligible for SSI

Figure 3. SSA's Sequential Evaluation Process for Childhood Disabilities

72

follow in evaluating childhood disability. Table 23 identifies the relevant assessment domains.

The *Zebley* decision impacts determinations of childhood disability in two ways. First, a functional assessment now must be a part of all determinations of childhood disability. Second, children who applied for and were denied SSI benefits between January 1, 1980, and February 11, 1991, must be notified of their right to be reevaluated under the functional assessment standard and, if found to be eligible, are entitled to receive retroactive SSI benefits to the date of application.

Retroactive Benefits. Approximately 510,000 children were within the class of *Zebley* children whom SSA was required to contact and reevaluate for SSI eligibility under the functional assessment standard. If an individual had an impairment at the time of the reevaluation and there was no medical evidence to the contrary, SSA presumed that the same impairment existed at the time the individual originally applied. SSA also presumed, in the absence of evidence to the contrary, that the individual met the income and resources requirements for the time period under consideration, as long as it was between 1980 and 1990.

The* Zebley *Decision and Medicaid. States have been encouraged to provide retroactive Medicaid benefits to children who are found to be eligible for retroactive SSI benefits under *Zebley,* but they have not been required to do so. HCFA has notified states of their option to provide retroactive Medicaid benefits and the availability of Federal Financial Par-

Table 23. Functional Criteria: SSA Assessment Domains for Childhood Disability

Age	Consider
Less than one	▪ Responsiveness to stimuli ▪ Motor ▪ Cognitive ▪ Communicative ▪ Social
One to three	▪ Motor ▪ Cognitive ▪ Communicative ▪ Social ▪ Personal and behavioral development
Three to 18	▪ Cognitive ▪ Communicative ▪ Motor ▪ Social ▪ Personal /Behavioral ▪ Concentration, persistence, and pace

ticipation (FFP) if a state opts to do so. FFP will be available for retroactive Medicaid benefits and for medical assistance benefits paid by states to *Zebley* children during the retroactive period.

The Childhood Listing of Mental Impairments

Revised in December 1990, the Childhood Listing of Mental Impairments used by SSA to determine childhood disability incorporates functional criteria as required under *Zebley* and greatly expands the range of mental disorders that qualify a child for SSI. Evaluations must include both clinical findings and an assessment of the limitations on the child's basic functioning. Conditions now considered disabling that previously were not included in the mental impairments listing include nonmosaic Down syndrome, PKU, fetal alcohol syndrome, and autism. Table 24 shows the new categories of childhood mental impairments under the revised listing.

SSI and HIV Infection

On December 17, 1991, SSA issued a notice of its new ruling on Human Immunodeficiency Virus (HIV) infection as a disabling condition for Social Security purposes. The ruling revises and expands the guidelines for evaluating HIV infection. Specifically, the ruling includes additional criteria to take into account the clinical manifestations and course of HIV infection in women and children, criteria not previously outlined in SSA guidelines. The ruling addresses

Table 24. SSI Categories of Childhood Mental Impairments (Revised)

- Organic mental disorders
- Schizophrenic, delusional (paranoid), schizoaffective, and other psychotic disorders
- Mood disorders
- Mental retardation
- Anxiety disorders
- Somatoform, eating, and tic disorders
- Personality disorders
- Psychoactive substance dependence disorders
- Autistic disorders and other pervasive developmental disorders
- Attention deficit hyperactivity disorders
- Developmental and emotional disorders of newborns and young infants (birth to age 1)

documentation of HIV infection in children, identifies special evaluation issues for children with HIV infection, and details the manifestations of HIV infection in children.

Representative Payment

All payments for children who are disabled and entitled to SSI benefits are made to representative payees. The payee is usually the parent, but other individuals or entities—including public and private child welfare and other social service agencies—may apply to become the representative payee for a child. Representative payees are required to use SSI payments only for the child's current and foreseeable needs and must periodically account to SSA for how the benefits were used. SSA determines who will act as a child's representative payee.

Chapter 7
Title IV-A: Aid to Families with Dependent Children (AFDC)

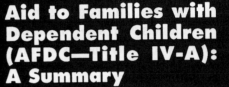

Aid to Families with Dependent Children (AFDC—Title IV-A): A Summary

Nature of Program
Provides states with funds for income support for eligible families with dependent children. Children must be under 18, living with a "caretaker relative," and deprived of parental support or care. Pregnant women without other children may be eligible if the child, when born, would be AFDC eligible. Support levels vary by state and family size.

Funding Type
Entitlement. State match varies according to the state's relative per capita income.

For More Information
Office of Family Assistance, Administration for Children and Families, U.S. Department of Health and Human Services, Aerospace Building, 5th Floor, 370 L'Enfant Promenade, SW, Washington, DC 20447. Phone: 202/401–9275.

AFDC, administered by the Administration for Children and Families, U.S. Department of Health and Human Services, is an income support program that provides cash grants for basic maintenance to eligible needy families if and for as long as the family includes a "dependent child" (defined by federal standards), and the family is financially eligible (defined by state standards). Maximum AFDC benefits vary by state, as shown in table 25.

Like Medicaid, AFDC is a federal/state partnership, in which all states participate. The federal government reimburses each state on the basis of a statutory formula that takes into account the state's per capita income in relation to the national per capita income. The minimum federal reimbursement is 50 percent of the state's AFDC program costs; the maximum rate is 83 percent. Table 26 sets out the federal participation rates for FY 1994 for each state participating in AFDC.

AFDC is an entitlement program that operates at two levels. States, upon complying with federal requirements for the program, are entitled to federal reimbursement for the costs incurred in implementing their AFDC programs. The federal government guarantees that it will match, at a specific rate, state AFDC expenditures irrespective of the total costs incurred. Similarly, eligible families are entitled to AFDC benefits because states are required to provide benefits to all eligible individuals who apply.

Eligibility Requirements

To qualify for AFDC benefits, an individual must meet status requirements, financial requirements, and conduct requirements.

Status Requirements

Federal rules specify the categories of individuals who are eligible for AFDC. AFDC benefits are available for:

- *Dependent children*, who, under federal law, must be (1) under the age of 18, (2) living with a "caretaker relative," and (3) deprived of parental support or care.

- *Caretaker relatives*, who, under federal law, include the following: father, mother, grandfather, grandmother, brother, sister, stepfather, stepmother, stepbrother, stepsister, uncle, aunt, first cousin, nephew or niece; persons of previous generations whose relationships with the child is preceded by the prefixes of grand- great-, or great-great-; and the spouses of any of the relatives listed.

- *Pregnant women*, who, even if not otherwise eligible for AFDC, under federal law may be covered from the sixth month of pregnancy if the fetus would be eligible for AFDC if it were a child.

Federal law also requires that an individual who receives AFDC benefits be a citizen, an alien lawfully admitted for permanent residence, or an alien permanently residing in the U.S. under color of law. Under federal law, states may exclude from eligibility nonresidents, certain families headed by minor parents, and recipients who are currently receiving SSI benefits.

Financial Requirements

Financial eligibility is determined on the basis of the *AFDC assistance unit*, which usually comprises a caretaker relative and one or more dependent children. Through a complex set of rules, "gross income" is determined, as well as "countable income and resources," to assess eligibility for AFDC benefits and the amount of the benefit when the family is eligible.

Conduct Requirements

Under federal law, AFDC recipients may be required, as a condition of eligibility, to refrain from or to engage in certain activities. They may not participate in a strike or to engage in any fraudulent conduct in relationship to AFDC benefits, and must furnish or apply for a social security number, participate in work programs, and cooperate with child support collection activities.

AFDC Program Administration

To receive federal funding for AFDC, a state must submit to the U.S. Department of Health and Human Services a plan that demonstrates full compliance with federal AFDC requirements. Each state must designate a single state agency to either directly administer the AFDC program or supervise its administration by local government agencies. The majority of states have state-agency-administered AFDC programs. Some states, however, including Alabama, California, Colorado, Georgia, Maryland, Minnesota, Montana, New Jersey, New York, North Carolina, North Dakota, Ohio, South Carolina, Virginia, and Wisconsin, have state-supervised, locally administered programs.

The AFDC Administrative Process

AFDC program administration is subject to extensive federal regulation. Some of the federal regulations that govern the AFDC administrative process are:

- *The application process:* Notice of the application decision, and the first check to the recipient if the application is approved, must be mailed within 45 days of the date of application.
- *Appeals:* There is a right to appeal adverse decisions regarding AFDC benefits to a state agency "fair hearing."
- *Overpayments:* States have the right to recover all AFDC overpayments, even those resulting from agency error.
- *Underpayments:* All AFDC underpayments must be corrected, including those made to former AFDC recipients who are no longer eligible for AFDC benefits.
- *Method of payment:* Benefits are to be paid directly to the caretaker relative, with no restriction on their use.

Table 25. Maximum AFDC Benefits by Family Size, January 1993*

State	2-person Family	3-person Family	4-person Family	5-person Family	6-person Family
Alabama	$137	$164	$194	$225	$252
Alaska	821	923	1,025	1,127	1,229
Arizona	275	347	418	489	561
Arkansas	162	204	247	286	331
California	504	624	743	847	952
Colorado	280	356	432	512	590
Connecticut	549	680	792	893	999
Delaware	270	338	407	475	544
District of Columbia	321	409	499	575	676
Florida	241	303	364	426	487
Georgia	235	280	330	378	410
Guam	258	330	417	497	592
Hawaii	550	693	835	978	1,121
Idaho	254	315	357	399	433
Illinois	268	367	414	485	545
Indiana	229	288	346	405	463
Iowa	361	426	495	548	610
Kansas	352	429	497	558	619
Kentucky	196	228	285	333	376
Louisiana	138	190	234	277	316
Maine	337	453	569	685	801
Maryland	280	359	432	501	551
Massachusetts	446	539	628	720	814
Michigan					
Washtenaw County	401	489	593	689	822
Wayne County	371	459	563	659	792
Minnesota	437	532	621	697	773
Mississippi	96	120	144	168	192
Missouri	234	292	342	388	431
Montana	310	390	470	550	630

Table 25. Maximum AFDC Benefits by Family Size, January 1993 (Continued)

State	2-person Family	3-person Family	4-person Family	5-person Family	6-person Family
Nebraska	$293	$364	$435	$506	$577
Nevada	289	348	407	466	525
New Hampshire	451	516	575	631	707
New Jersey	322	424	488	552	616
New Mexico	258	324	389	455	520
New York					
Suffolk County	576	703	824	949	1,038
New York City	468	577	687	800	884
North Carolina	236	272	297	324	349
North Dakota	326	401	491	558	616
Ohio	279	341	421	493	549
Oklahoma	251	324	402	470	538
Oregon	395	460	565	660	755
Pennsylvania	330	421	514	607	687
Puerto Rico	156	180	204	228	252
Rhode Island	449	554	632	710	800
South Carolina	159	200	240	281	321
South Dakota	357	404	450	497	543
Tennessee	142	185	226	264	305
Texas	158	184	221	246	284
Utah	323	402	470	536	589
Vermont	554	659	740	829	887
Virgin Islands	180	240	300	360	420
Virginia	294	354	410	488	518
Washington	440	546	642	740	841
West Virginia	201	249	312	360	413
Wyoming	440	517	617	708	766
Wisconsin	320	360	390	450	510
Median State Benefit	310	367	435	506	577

* U.S. House of Representatives Committee on Ways and Means, *Overview of Entitlement Programs: 1991 Green Book* (Washington, DC: U.S. Government Printing Office, 1991), p. 130.

Table 26. Federal Percentages for the AFDC Program (FY 1994)

State	Federal Percentage	State	Federal Percentage
Alabama	65.00	Montana	65.00
Alaska	50.00	Nebraska	57.76
American Samoa	50.00	Nevada	50.00
Arizona	62.11	New Hampshire	50.00
Arkansas	65.00	New Jersey	50.00
California	50.00	New Mexico	65.00
Colorado	50.00	New York	50.00
Connecticut	50.00	North Carolina	61.26
Delaware	50.00	North Dakota	65.00
District of Columbia	50.00	Northern Mariana	50.00
Florida	50.00	Ohio	56.48
Georgia	58.30	Oklahoma	65.00
Guam	50.00	Oregon	57.21
Hawaii	50.00	Pennsylvania	50.00
Idaho	65.00	Puerto Rico	50.00
Illinois	50.00	Rhode Island	50.00
Indiana	59.43	South Carolina	65.00
Iowa	59.26	South Dakota	65.00
Kansas	55.02	Tennessee	63.50
Kentucky	65.00	Texas	60.20
Louisiana	65.00	Utah	65.00
Maine	57.73	Vermont	55.06
Maryland	50.00	Virgin Islands	50.00
Massachusetts	50.00	Virginia	50.00
Michigan	51.52	Washington	50.00
Minnesota	50.00	West Virginia	65.00
Mississippi	65.00	Wisconsin	56.06
Missouri	56.26	Wyoming	61.82

Chapter 8
Other Income
Support Programs

Two other income support programs that may provide significant benefits for children and families are the Title IV-A Emergency Assistance Program and the Title IV-D Child Support Enforcement Program.

Title IV-A Emergency Assistance

States, at their option, may include an Emergency Assistance Program as part of their Aid to Families with Dependent Children (AFDC) program. Emergency Assistance is designed to meet the crisis needs of families with children. Such assistance must be necessary to avoid the destitution of the child or to provide a child with living arrangements in a home. Each state must submit its Emergency Assistance Program plan to and obtain approval from the U.S. Department of Health and Human Services (HHS). When a state includes emergency assistance within its AFDC program, AFDC-eligible families may apply for and receive emergency assistance benefits. States also have the option of extending Title IV-A emergency assistance benefits to non-AFDC eligible families.

Eligibility

Under federal regulations, eligibility for emergency assistance is based on meeting a minimum of four criteria:

1. The family has a needy child under 21 years of age.

2. The needy child lives with an appropriate relative or has lived with such a relative within six months prior to application.

3. The family is without resources immediately accessible to meet its needs.

4. The need for emergency assistance has not arisen because the child or the child's relative refused to accept employment or training without good cause.

Services

Services to any family under Title IV-A Emergency Assistance may be provided for a specified period of time as outlined in the state's Emergency Assistance plan as approved by HHS. Emergency assistance may be made available to cover a wide variety of emergencies, including homelessness, eviction, utility shut-off, and appliance breakdown. States have flexibility in the emergencies they opt to cover and in the services they offer to meet such emergencies. Services may include direct cash payments to families for rent or utility bills; shelter, housing, or housing referral; and specific items such as food, clothing, and furniture. A growing number of states are making use of emergency assistance funds to shelter families or prevent evictions.

Federal Matching

The federal financial participation rate is 50 percent of the state's emergency assistance payments. Under prior practice, the federal government limited its financial participation to the payments made to any one family during one period of 30 consecutive days in any 12 months. Recent interpretations of this rule by regional offices of the U.S. Department of Health and Human Ser-

Title IV-A Emergency Assistance: A Summary

Nature of Program

Optional program that states may offer with the AFDC program. It enables states to meet crisis needs of families with children. A family may receive assistance for a specified period of time in any 12-month period. A broad array of services may be provided, including direct cash payments for rent, services, and food.

Funding Type

Yearly appropriation. State match is 50 percent.

For More Information

Office of Family Assistance, Administration for Children and Families, U.S. Department of Health and Human Services, Aerospace Building, 5th Floor, 370 L'Enfant Promenade, SW, Washington, DC 20447. Phone: 202/401–9275.

vices, however, have permitted federal participation for longer periods of time, such as three months or six months, if the extended services are determined to be necessary during the 30-day assessment period to address the crisis, and the state opts to provide services over a longer period of time.

Funding Level
For FY 1992, $176.9 million was appropriated for the Emergency Assistance Program; for FY 1993, $155 million was appropriated.

Title IV-D: The Child Support Provisions of the Family Support Act

Under federal law, states that participate in AFDC must have in place a child support enforcement program that complies with Title IV-D of the Social Security Act. Each state's Title IV-D program is charged with locating absent parents, establishing paternity when necessary, obtaining and modifying support orders, and enforcing child support orders.

Eligible Families
Individuals who receive AFDC ("AFDC IV-D families") are automatically eligible for Title IV-D services and must receive them without charge. Families that receive Medicaid but not AFDC ("Medicaid-only IV-D families") are eligible for child support enforcement services with no fee. Families that lose eligibility for AFDC ("post-AFDC families") may receive some Title IV-D services without paying a fee, but may be required to pay for other services. Those families who simply need child support assistance ("non-AFDC families") may file an application with the state Title IV-D agency and may be required to pay an application fee and fees for certain services These latter families are entitled to services upon payment of the requested fees.

Title IV-D Child Support Provisions of the Family Support Act of 1988: A Summary

Nature of Program
Provides funding to states to enforce child support payments by absentee parents. Up to $50 of each collected payment goes to the family, with no effect on the AFDC benefit. The balance goes first to reimburse the state and federal governments for AFDC and then to the family.

Funding Type
States pay one-third of the costs of administering the program and receive incentive payments for successful collection.

For More Information
Office of Child Support Enforcement, Administration for Children and Families, U.S. Department of Health and Human Services, Aerospace Building, 370 L'Enfant Promenade, SW, 6th Floor, Washington, DC 20447. Phone: 202/401–9370

Funding

To receive federal Title IV-D funds, a state must submit a state plan that demonstrates compliance with 23 different criteria. Upon approval of the plan by the Office of Child Support Enforcement in the U.S. Department of Health and Human Services, the federal government pays 66 percent of the basic costs of the Title IV-D program. States also receive incentive payments for successful collection of child support. The incentive payment ranges from six to ten percent of the support collected. Limits on incentive payments vary with the type of family for whom support is collected. For AFDC IV-D families, there is no limit on the incentive pay-ments that a state may receive. For all other families (Medicaid-only IV-D families, post-AFDC families, and non-AFDC families), however, the total incentive payment may not be greater than 115 percent of the incentive payment for AFDC families.

Distribution of Support Collections

The distribution of support collections between the government and the family is subject to complex federal requirements and will vary depending on the type of family for whom support is collected. Table 28 summarizes the Title IV-D child support enforcement rules for the four types of families served under Title IV-D.

Table 28. Title IV-D Child Support Enforcement Services

Family Category	Eligibility for Services	Distribution of Support Collections
AFDC IV-D families	Automatic eligibility; no charge for services	1. Pass-through of first $50 to family 2. Reimbursement to federal and state governments of AFDC benefit paid that month 3. Excess support to family up to current support obligation 4. Arrears payments to state or family
Medicaid-only IV-D families	Automatic eligibility; no charge for services	1. Reimbursement to the Medicaid agency for services paid by Medicaid 2. Reimbursement by Medicaid agency to custodial parent if he/she paid for the medical care
Post-AFDC families	Must apply for services; may be required to pay for certain services	1. Payment to family to meet current support obligation 2. Arrears payments at state option: client arrears or AFDC arrears
Non-AFDC families	Must apply for services; may be required to pay application fee and to pay for certain services	Family receives all collected support

AFDC Families. For AFDC families, several distribution steps are involved. The first $50 that is collected goes to the family. This amount, called a *pass-through,* is added to the family's usual AFDC benefit and does not affect AFDC eligibility.

Next, the state and the federal government are both reimbursed for the AFDC benefit that each paid to the family that month. If money remains, the family receives additional funds (called *excess support)* up to the amount of the support obligation for the current month. If money still remains, the state keeps the remaining funds to repay itself for any arrears owed the state under AFDC. If there are no such arrears, the money is used to pay arrears owed to the child's custodian (*arrears payments*).

Both excess support and arrears payments to families may affect the family's AFDC eligibility and level of benefit. When such payments contribute to a family's ineligibility for AFDC, the family is considered—for the purpose of Medicaid eligibility only—to be receiving AFDC for a peri-od of four calendar months after the last month of AFDC eligibility.

Medicaid-Only IV-D Families. Medicaid-only cases usually involve collecting money from an insurance company to reimburse claims already paid by Medicaid. If, however, money is collected directly from an absent parent, the money will first go to the state Medicaid agency as reimbursement for provided services. If the custodial parent paid for the medical care, the Medicaid agency is required to reimburse the custodial parent.

Post-AFDC Families. Support obligations are first counted as a payment on the obligation for the current month. Any amount received in excess of the current month's obligation is treated as payments on arrears. Some states have a policy that the money first pays client arrears, then AFDC arrears. Other states give priority to AFDC arrears. States may not keep any collection as attributable to AFDC arrears. All collections must first be given to the family to meet the current support obligation.

Non-AFDC IV-D Cases. A non-AFDC family receives all support collected.

Section IV
Additional Sources
of Federal Funding

Sections I through III provide a look at the major sources of government money for child welfare services. Section IV describes federal funding services for an array of other programs: child day care services; nutritional services; health, mental health, and substance abuse services; juvenile justice services; and education.

Chapter 9
Child Day Care Funding

Federal programs that provide funds for child day care include the Child Care and Development Block Grant, At-Risk Child Care under Title IV-A of the Social Security Act, the JOBS Child Care and Transitional Child Care programs under Title IV-A of the Social Security Act, and the Temporary Child Care for Children with Disabilities and Crisis Nurseries program administered by the Administration for Children and Families of the U.S. Department of Health and Human Services. Other programs that benefit child day care include the State Dependent Care and Development grants, the Child Care Food Program, the Dependent Care Tax Credit, and the Social Services Block Grant (Title XX), which is used by many states as a funding source for child day care services.

The Child Care and Development Block Grant

The Child Care and Development Block Grant provides funds to states for child care services and activities to increase the availability, affordability, and quality of child day care. Final regulations for the program specifically emphasize parental choice of day care and require that states make certificates (vouchers) available as one option, among others, to maximize parental choice. Parents may choose from a variety of child care providers, including child care centers, group home providers, family child care providers, sectarian organizations, relatives, friends, and neighbors.

Funding

The Block Grant authorizes $825 million for FY 1992, $925 million for FY 1993, and such sums as deemed necessary by Congress for FY 1994 and FY 1995. For FY 1993, Congress appropriated $892.8 million and for FY 1994, $892.7 million. These funds are released to the states upon approval by HHS of each state's child care plan.

Each state's funding under the Block Grant is determined by a formula that includes the number of children younger than age five in the state, the number of children receiving free and reduced-price school lunches, and the state's per capita income. Up to 3 percent of the Block Grant is set aside for grants and/or contracts with Native American tribes and tribal organizations, and 0.5 percent is reserved for the territories, including Guam, American Samoa, the U.S. Virgin Islands, the Northern Marianas, and the Pacific Trust Territory. For allocation purposes, the District of Columbia and Puerto Rico are considered states.

States are not required to provide matching funds in order to receive federal funds under the Block Grant. A state may carry over part or all of a previous fiscal year's funding to the next two fiscal years. This factor is critical, since the FY 1991 and subsequent appropriations bills have specified that the funds not be available until the end of each fiscal year, constituting, in effect, advance funding for the next year's program.

Use of Funds

States that receive Block Grant funds must spend 75 percent of the funds on child care services and activities to improve the availability and quality of child care; 85 percent of that amount must go toward child care services. Of the remaining 25 percent,

The Child Care and Development Block Grant: A Summary

Nature of Program
Provides funding through block grants to the states for day care services for children in low-income families. Priority must be given to children in very low-income families and those with special needs. Parents must be working or attending a job training or educational program.

Funding Type
Yearly appropriations. A state match is not required.

For More Information
Administration for Children and Families, U.S. Department of Health and Human Services, Aerospace Building, 370 L'Enfant Promenade, SW, 5th Floor, Washington, DC 20447. Phone: 202/205–8347.

states must spend 75 percent for early childhood development and/or before- and after-school services; 20 percent on improving the quality of child care; and the remaining 5 percent on any activity permitted under the legislation. Quality-improvement activities include:

- Developing, establishing, expanding, operating, or coordinating resource and referral services.

- Providing grants or loans to help providers meet applicable state and local standards.

- Monitoring compliance with licensing and regulatory requirements.

- Providing training and technical assistance in areas appropriate to the provision of child care services, such as training in health and safety, nutrition, first aid, the recognition of communicable diseases, child abuse detection and

prevention, and the care of children with special needs.

- Improving salaries and benefits of staff members (full- and part-time) who provide child care in funded programs.

Figure 4 sets forth the requirements for use of funds under the Block Grant. Federal funds must be used only to supplement, not to supplant, the amount of state and local funds spent for child care services and related programs.

Eligibility

Families are eligible to receive child care assistance under the Block Grant if their children are younger than age 13 and if their family income is less than 75 percent of the state median income; states, however, have the option of restricting eligibility to families at lower income levels. Priority is to be given to children in very low-income families and to children with special needs. Parents must be work-

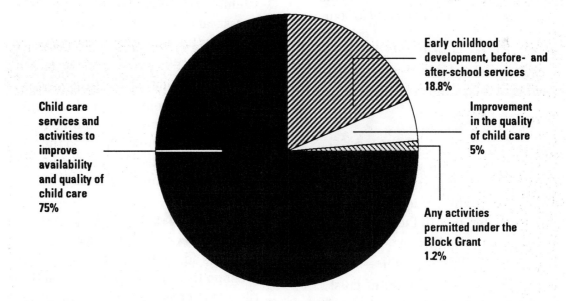

Child care services and activities to improve availability and quality of child care 75%

Early childhood development, before- and after-school services 18.8%

Improvement in the quality of child care 5%

Any activities permitted under the Block Grant 1.2%

Figure 4. The Child Care and Development Block Grant: Requirements for States' Use of Funds

ing or attending a job training or educational program. Benefits from other federal programs are not counted against a family's income when determining eligibility. Children who are receiving or need to receive protective services and those in foster care are also eligible for child care assistance. A child in foster care may be considered as a "family of one" for purposes of determining income eligibility.

Administration
Each state's governor must select a lead agency to administer the child care activities supported under the Block Grant. The lead agency is required to coordinate the Block Grant with other federal, state, and local child care programs.

States must prepare an initial plan covering a three-year period and subsequent plans for a two-year period. In conjunction with the development of the state plan, the lead agency must hold at least one hearing in the state to provide the public with an opportunity to comment on the provision of child day care services under the state plan. States must consult with local governments in the drafting of their child care plans.

Child Care Providers
Before they can receive Block Grant funds, child care providers must comply with applicable state and local requirements and be licensed, regulated, or registered with the state (for those in states that lack licensing requirements or regulation).

1. The registration procedures must enable states to give providers information about available health and safety training, technical assistance, and state regulatory requirements.

2. Providers must be able to register after being selected by parents of eligible children.

3. Providers 18 years of age and over who care for grandchildren, nieces, or nephews must be registered, but are not required to comply with any state or local child care requirements.

4. All providers receiving funds under the act must meet a set of specific health and safety requirements imposed by the state. Standards must address prevention and control of infectious disease, including immunization; building and physical premises safety requirements; and health and safety training for providers appropriate to each provider's setting.

5. States may impose requirements more stringent than federal requirements on child care providers who receive assistance under the Block Grant, as long as the state requirements do not adversely affect parental choice.

6. If a state reduces licensing or regulatory requirements for child care providers, it must explain its reasons in its annual report to the Secretary of the U.S. Department of Health and Human Services.

Title IV-A: Child Care for At-Risk Children
Congress added the At-Risk Child Care program to Title IV-A of the Social Security Act to create a child care program for low-income working families who

are not receiving Aid to Families with Dependent Children (AFDC). This optional program permits states to provide child care to families who need it in order to work and who otherwise would be at risk of becoming dependent on AFDC. States have complete discretion in developing the criteria that place an individual or family at risk, and may use income alone as the criterion.

Funding

At-Risk Child Care funding is a capped entitlement and does not require an annual appropriation by Congress. The authorization level is set at $300 million each year for FY 1991 through FY 1995.

State funding allocations are determined by a formula that includes the ratio of the number of children under age 13 residing in the state to the number of children under age 13 in the entire United States. Funds are directed to the state agency that administers programs under the Family Support Act of 1988, including the JOBS program.

The federal participation rate for the Title IV-A At-Risk Child Care Program is the same as the state's Medicaid match rate. The state match may be met with state or local funds, but not with federal funds such as those from Title XX (the Social Services Block Grant). At-risk child day care funds may not be used to supplant any state or local funds expended for child care services. States may carry over funds from one fiscal year to the next, but if they do so, they are required to spend all of the current year's allotment before spending funds carried over from the previous year.

Administration

States have considerable latitude in implementing the program. They may opt to provide care directly; arrange care through private child day care providers by purchase of service contracts or grants; provide cash or vouchers in advance to the family; reimburse the family; or adopt other arrangements the state deems appropriate. States, however, must make vouchers available as one of the parental options.

At-Risk Child Care for Low-Income Children (Title IV-A): A Summary

Nature of Program

Provides funding to states for child day care for families who are at risk of becoming dependent on AFDC and who need child care in order to work.

Funding Type

Capped entitlement. State match is the same as the Medicaid matching rate.

For More Information

Administration for Children and Families, U.S. Department of Health and Human Services, Aerospace Building, 370 L'Enfant Promenade, SW, 5th Floor, Washington, DC 20447. Phone: 202/205–8347.

Providers must be paid the amount that is the lesser of (1) the actual cost of care or (2) the 75th percentile of the local market rate. Under this program, states may require providers to meet basic health and safety standards applicable to other federal- or state-subsidized child care programs. Unless a provider provides care solely to relatives, the provider must be licensed, regulated, or registered.

Eligibility

Families are eligible for child care assistance under the At-Risk Child Care program if they are not receiving AFDC, need child care in order to work, and are determined by the state to be at risk of becoming dependent on AFDC.

JOBS and Transitional Child Care

Title IV-A contains two additional provisions for child care: (1) child care during participation in Title IV-F JOBS work, education, or job training or an approved self-initiated education or training program; and (2) transitional child care assistance as individuals move from AFDC eligibility to employment status.

1. *Child care during participation in work, education, or training.* The state agency that administers the AFDC program must guarantee child care if it determines that child care is necessary for an individual's participation in education, training, and employment activities, including the JOBS program and individually initiated employment, training, or education; if the activity is approved; and if the individual is participating satisfactorily.

2. *Transitional child care assistance.* The second component of the child day care program under Title IV-A is

JOBS and Transitional Child Care (Title IV-A): A Summary

Nature of Program
Provides funds to states for daytime care for children of participants in Title IV-F JOBS work, education, and job training programs or an approved self-initiated education or training program. Under Transitional Child Care, up to 12 months of child care must be provided when the family has become ineligible for AFDC because of employment.

Funding Type
Entitlement. State match is the same as the Medicaid matching rate.

For More Information
Administration for Children and Families, U.S. Department of Health and Human Services, Aerospace Building, 370 L'Enfant Promenade, SW, 5th Floor, Washington, DC 20447. Phone: 202/401–9326.

designed to enhance a parent's transition from AFDC to employment. Under the rules for Transitional Child Care Assistance, child care must be provided when the state agency determines that it is necessary for an individual's employment and the family has become ineligible for AFDC because of increased hours of employment, increased income from employment, or lost earnings disregards. Child care is limited to 12 months after the last month in which the family received AFDC assistance. Families are required to contribute to their own child care expenses as their income increases, and states must establish sliding fee scales based on the ability of the family to pay.

Funding
The child care assistance provided under Title IV-A JOBS and Transitional Child Care is funded as an uncapped entitlement. The federal matching rate is the same as the state's Medicaid matching rate.

Provision of Services
Under the JOBS and Transitional Child Care Assistance Programs, the state agency may provide child day care itself, arrange care by use of contracts or vouchers, provide cash or vouchers in advance to the caretaker relative, reimburse the caretaker relative, or adopt any other arrangements deemed appropriate by the agency. Emphasis, however, is placed on vouchers to maximize parental choice. Reimbursement for the cost of care may not be less than the amount of the child care disregard for which the family is otherwise eligible under AFDC nor more than the 75th percentile of the local market rate, regardless of the method selected to provide care.

The Temporary Child Care for Children with Disabilities and Crisis Nurseries Program
The Temporary Child Care for Children with Disabilities and Crisis Nurseries

Temporary Child Care for Children with Disabilities and Crisis Nurseries Program: A Summary

Nature of Program
Provides discretionary grants to states for temporary nonmedical child care for children with disabilities or chronic illnesses, including HIV and AIDS. Also provides for crisis nurseries for abused or neglected children.

Funding Type
Yearly appropriation; 25 percent state match.

For More Information
Children's Bureau, Program Support Division, Administration for Children and Families, U.S. Department of Health and Human Services, 330 C Street, SW, Washington, DC 20201. Phone: 202/205–8347.

Act of 1986 provides grants to states to assist public and private agencies in developing two types of programs—respite care and crisis nurseries.

Respite Care

Respite care funds may be used to provide in-home or out-of-home temporary nonmedical child care, or respite care, for children with disabilities and children with chronic or terminal illnesses, including children with HIV/AIDS or AIDS-related conditions.

These temporary child care programs for children with disabilities or children who are chronically or terminally ill must be designed to alleviate the families' social, economic, and financial stress. Programs must provide families or primary caregivers with periods of temporary relief from the pressures of child care.

Crisis Nurseries

Crisis nurseries are child care facilities that provide temporary emergency services and care for abused or neglected children, children at risk of abuse and neglect, or children in families receiving protective services. These programs are designed to develop a safe environment as a resource for children at risk of abuse or neglect; deliver nonpunitive, nonthreatening services as a resource to caregivers of at-risk children; and utilize existing community-based services to reduce the potential for child maltreatment when families are experiencing a crisis.

Eligibility

This program is administered by the Administration for Children and Families of the U.S. Department of Health and Human Services. Only state agencies designated by the governor of the state to carry out programs funded under the Temporary Child Care for Children with Disabilities and Crisis Nurseries may apply for these grants. States, however, may contract with private providers to deliver the services. Applicants must specifically apply for either the Temporary Child Care for Children with Disabilities and Chronically Ill Children or the Crisis Nurseries Program and must:

1. Document the state's commitment to developing a state plan for coordination among agencies that serve children.

2. Describe the proposed state program to assist private and public agencies or organizations either to provide (a) in-home or out-of-home temporary, nonmedical care to children with disabilities and children with chronic or terminal illnesses, including drug-related conditions, and children with AIDS or AIDS-related conditions, or (b) crisis nurseries for abused and neglected children and children at risk of abuse or neglect.

3. Describe how funds previously awarded to the state under the program have been used and how the new funds would be used to enhance or expand existing programs.

4. Describe the services to be provided, the agencies and organizations that would provide the services, and the criteria that would be employed in the selection of children and families for participation in the project.

Projects may offer 24-hour emergency response services; access to primary medical services; referral to counseling/therapy services; staff training, including coverage of child abuse/neglect reporting responsibilities; and public awareness programs.

Funding

Funding is equally divided between the two programs, with consideration given to equitable geographic distribution. For FY 1993 and for FY 1994, $11.9 million was appropriated.

State grantees must provide 25 percent of the total project cost. The program was reauthorized at $20 million a year through FY 1995 by the Child Abuse, Domestic Violence, Adoption and Family Service Act of 1992 (P.L. 102-295).

Summary of Major Child Day Care Funding Programs

Table 28 compares the four major federal child day care funding programs described in this chapter.

Other Programs that Support Child Day Care Services

In addition to the programs described above, four other programs provide additional federal funding for child day care: State Dependent Care Development Grants, the Child Care Food Program, the Dependent Care Tax Credit, and the Title XX Social Services Block Grant.

State Dependent Care Development Grants

The State Dependent Care Development Grant program provides federal matching funds to help states plan, develop, establish, expand, improve, or operate before- and after-school child care programs for school-age children and resource and referral systems that provide information on dependent care services. For FY 1994, $12.9 million has been appropriated. Funds are allocated to states on the basis of state population as a percentage of the total population of the United States, except that no state may receive less than $50,000 in any fiscal year. The program is administered at the federal level by the Administration for Children and Families of the U.S. Department of Health and Human Services, and is authorized through FY 1994 by the Augustus Hawkins Human Services Reauthorization Act of 1990 (P.L. 101-501).

For more information, contact: Administration for Children and Families, U.S. Department of Health and Human Services, Aerospace Building, 370 L'Enfant Promenade, SW, 5th Floor, Washington, DC 20447. Phone: 202/205–8347.

Child Care Food Program

The Child Care Food program is permanently authorized under the National School Lunch Act of 1946. The program provides federal financial assistance for meals and snacks served to children from low-income families in licensed

Table 28. Major Federal Child Day Care Funding Programs

Program	Type	Eligible Families	Required Categories of Care	Payment Rates	Federal Match	FY 1993 Funding	FY 1994 Funding
						(in millions of dollars)	
Child Care and Development Block Grant	Block Grant (amount appropriated each year)	Low-income families with children under age 13	■ Center-based ■ Group home ■ Family child care	Must meet two requirements: ■ 75th percentile of local market rates ■ Not significantly restrictive of parent choice	100 percent	$892.8	$892.7
Title IV-A At-Risk Child Care	Capped entitlement	Non-AFDC-eligible families defined by state as being "at risk"	■ Center-based ■ Group home ■ Family child care ■ In-home care	75th percentile of local market rates or lower statewide rate	Medicaid match rate	$300	$300
Title IV-A JOBS and Transitional Child Care	Uncapped entitlement	■ AFDC-eligible individuals participating in work, education, training, or JOBS ■ Previously AFDC-eligible individuals who are moving into employment status	Not applicable	Floor of $175 a month for a child over age 2, $200 a month for a child under age 2, sliding fee scale for transitional year	Medicaid match rate	Not applicable	Not applicable
Temporary Child Care and Crisis Nurseries	Discretionary grant program (amount appropriated each year)	Grantees must be designated state agencies; projects must serve families of children with disabilities, chronically ill children, or children at risk of abuse or neglect	Not applicable	Not specified in federal law or regulations	75 percent federal match	$11.9	$11.9

child care centers and family or group day care homes. The program is administered at the federal level by the Food and Nutrition Service of the U.S. Department of Agriculture.

For more information, contact: Director, Child Nutrition Division, Food and Nutrition Service, U.S. Department of Agriculture, Alexandria, VA 22302. Phone: 703/756–3590.

Dependent Care Tax Credit

Under Section 21 of the Internal Revenue Code, a nonrefundable credit against income tax liability is available for up to 30 percent of a limited amount of employment-related dependent care expenses. The maximum credit is $2,400 per year for one child and $4,800 for two children or more. The percentage used to calculate the credit depends on the taxpayer's adjusted gross income and is calculated on a sliding scale. A taxpayer whose adjusted gross income is $10,000 or less is allowed a credit equal to 30 percent of qualified expenditures. The credit percentage is reduced by one percent for each additional $2,000 of adjusted gross income above $10,000. For taxpayers whose income is greater then $28,000, the credit is equal to 20 percent of qualified expenses, up to the maximum credit.

For more information, contact: Director, Taxpayer Service Division, Internal Revenue Service, 1111 Constitution Avenue, NW, Room 7331, Washington, DC 20224. Phone 202/566–6352.

Title XX Social Services Block Grant

Title XX of the Social Security Act, discussed more fully in chapter 4, provides grants to states for a broad range of social services. A majority of states spend some portion of their grants on child care services. Title XX funds are provided to states on the basis of population, and no state match is required. States determine income eligibility levels and what services to provide.

For more information, contact: Director, Office of Policy, Planning and Legislation, Administration for Children and Families, U.S. Department of Health and Human Services, 300 Independence Avenue, SW, Washington, DC 20201. Phone: 202/245–2892.

Chapter 10
Nutrition Programs

Three federal programs address the nutritional needs of children, women, and families: (1) the Special Supplemental Food Program for Women, Infants, and Children (WIC); (2) the Food Stamp Program; and (3) the School Lunch and Breakfast Program. In addition, child care institutions, among other service providers, are eligible to receive surplus food under the Food Donation Program.

Special Supplemental Food Program for Women, Infants, and Children (WIC): A Summary

Nature of Program
Formula grants to states for supplemental food and nutrition education to benefit pregnant, postpartum, and breast feeding women; infants; and children to age five. Most states have set income eligibility at 185 percent of poverty level.
Funding Type
Yearly appropriation.
For More Information
Supplemental Food Programs Division, Food and Nutrition Service, U.S. Department of Agriculture, Alexandria, VA 22302. Phone: 703/756–3746.

Special Supplemental Food Program for Women, Infants, and Children (WIC)

The WIC Program provides supplemental food and nutrition education to eligible pregnant, postpartum, and breast feeding women; to infants; and to children up to age five.

Eligibility

WIC services are offered at no cost to eligible individuals. Individuals are eligible for WIC if they meet the state's income standard or are automatically determined to be income-eligible on the basis of their own or a family member's participation in certain health and welfare programs. States have the option of setting income eligibility between 100 and 185 percent of the federal poverty level, provided that income eligibility is no lower than the level set by the state for free or reduced-price health services. Nearly all states have set income eligibility at 185 percent of the poverty level.

Individuals are also eligible if they are determined to be at nutritional risk. Nutritional risks for women include medical risks, such as anemia, weight extremes, maternal age, poor pregnancy history, and dietary risks. Table 29 lists the nutritional risk criteria for infants and children.

States often have not had sufficient funds to serve all eligible persons who apply for the program. Federal regulations require that states establish a nutritional-risk priority system to ensure that those who most need program resources receive them.

Table 29. WIC Nutritional Risk Factors for Infants and Children

Nutritional Risk Factors for Infants	Nutritional Risk Factors for Children
■ Infant at risk because mother was in WIC or medically at risk during pregnancy ■ Low birthweight ■ Congenital malformation ■ Multiple birth ■ Frequent respiratory/intestinal illness ■ Anemia ■ Underweight ■ Stunted height ■ Congenital disorders ■ Chronic disorders ■ Overweight ■ Inadequate dietary pattern ■ Premature birth ■ Child of mother who is alcohol or drug involved ■ Child of drug-addicted mother ■ Prevention of regression	■ Inadequate dietary pattern ■ Frequent respiratory/intestinal illness ■ Anemia ■ Underweight ■ Stunted height ■ Congenital disorders ■ Chronic disorders ■ Overweight ■ Failure to thrive

Administration

The Food and Nutrition Service of the U.S. Department of Agriculture administers the program nationally and a designated state agency, usually the state department of health, oversees the program at the state level. The WIC agency at the state level usually enters into contracts with local agencies to administer the program. Local agencies that administer the WIC program typically operate within local health departments, community health centers, or the public health system.

Funding

Congress annually sets the funding level for the WIC program, and available funds are allocated to the states on the basis of a formula that takes into account, among other factors, the number and percentage of eligible children and women who are being served. Table 30 provides the federal funding history for WIC.

The Food Stamp Program

The Food Stamp Program is a federal program designed to enhance the ability of low-income individuals to purchase nutritious food. Food stamps are coupons that may be used to purchase food at participating grocery stores. Sales tax may not be charged on these purchases.

Administration and Funding

The U.S. Department of Agriculture administers the food stamp program nationally; in each state, a designated agency operates the program. Each year, Congress appropriates funds for the Food Stamp Program. As reflected in Table 31, total federal spending for the program has increased each year. The federal government funds the full cost of food stamp benefits and approximately 50 percent of the administrative costs. States, and in some instances local governments, pay the remaining administrative costs.

Eligibility

Any individual who falls within the federal limits on income and resources may receive food stamps. Financial eligibility is tied to the federal poverty line. As a result, a household will not be eligible for food stamps if its net monthly income, after deductions, is above

The Food Stamp Program: A Summary

Nature of Program
Funds coupons that low-income eligible persons may use for the purchase of food.
Funding Type
Yearly appropriation.
For More Information
Deputy Administrator, Food Stamp Program, Food and Nutrition Services, U.S. Department of Agriculture, Alexandria, VA 22302. Phone: 703/756–3022.

100 percent of the poverty line. If a member of the household is elderly or disabled, however, the household may qualify for food stamps if the household gross income does not exceed 130 percent of the poverty line. The food stamp monthly income limits are recalculated as of October 1 of each year to take inflation into account.

Households may receive food stamps even if they are not eligible for other benefit programs An individual, however, may not receive food stamps if:

- anyone in the household is on strike;

- the individual is an illegal alien;

- the individual lives in a boarding school, a jail, or certain other institutions that serve meals;

- the individual receives SSI benefits and lives in California or Wisconsin;

- the individual is currently under a disqualification because of food stamp fraud; or

- the individual is currently under a program disqualification because of voluntarily leaving employment without good cause or because of failure to comply with food stamp employment and training requirements.

The National School Lunch and Breakfast Program

The School Lunch Program, permanently authorized by the National School Lunch Act of 1946, and the School Breakfast Program, permanently authorized by the Child Nutrition Act of 1966, are two important federal programs designed to meet the nutritional needs of children.

Table 30. The WIC Program: Participation and Federal Costs

Fiscal Year	Number of Women Participating	(in thousands of persons) Number of Infants Participating	Number of Children Participating	(in billions of dollars) Funding
1986	712.0	945.0	1,655.0	$1.5
1987	751.0	1,019.0	1,660.0	$1.6
1988	815.0	1,095.0	1,683.0	$1.8
1989	951.8	1,259.6	1,907.0	$1.9
1990	1,034.4	1,411.9	2,065.0	$2.1
1991	1,120.1	1,558.8	2,213.8	$2.3
1992	1,221.5	1,684.1	2,505.2	$2.6
1993	Not Available	Not Available	Not Available	$2.9

The National School Lunch Program

The National School Lunch Program provides federal cash and commodity assistance to schools that serve lunches to students each school day. The program requires, among other things, that:

- lunches meet nutritional standards set by the U.S. Department of Agriculture;
- all children in the school have access to subsidized lunches;
- children from low-income families have the opportunity to receive free or reduced-price lunches; and
- the school does not make a profit on the lunch program.

Children with family incomes at or below 130 percent of the federal poverty level are eligible to receive free lunches. Those in families with incomes above 130 percent but at or below 185 percent of the poverty level are eligible to receive lunches at a reduced price. Children in families with incomes above 185 percent of the poverty level may receive lunches at the full, but still subsidized, price.

Eligible Schools. Schools eligible to participate in the lunch program are public elementary and secondary schools, and private, nonprofit elementary and secondary schools. Public and private, nonprofit licensed residential child care institutions, such as those that care for children with disabilities, and temporary homes for runaway children are also eligible to participate in the program.

Administration. The program is administered at the federal level by the Food and Nutrition Service of the U.S. Department of Agriculture. States usually administer the program through the state's educational agency.

Federal Funding. Federal assistance to states for the school lunch program is provided through cash or commodity reimbursement rates that are set by statute and adjusted for inflation each July 1. Federal cash reimbursement is

The National School Lunch and Breakfast Program: A Summary

Nature of Program
Cash and commodity assistance to schools to provide subsidized nutritious lunches and breakfasts for low-income children.

Funding Type
Yearly appropriation. The School Lunch Program requires a state match for the "basic assistance" portion of the program. No match is required for the School Breakfast Program.

For More Information
Director, Child Nutrition Division, Food and Nutrition Service, U.S. Department of Agriculture, Alexandria, VA 22302. Phone: 703/756–3590.

based on the number and type of meals served, with the amount of the federal cash reimbursement varying according to the family income of each participating child. All meals, however, are minimally subsidized through a "basic" reimbursement regardless of family income. In addition to the basic cash assistance, additional cash reimbursement is provided for each meal served to low-income children receiving free and reduced-price lunches.

State Match. State matching funds are required for federal funding provided under the basic assistance part of the program. These matching funds, in addition to contributions from local revenue and students' meal payments, are used to cover the full costs of operating the program. The school lunch program is the only child nutrition program that has requirements for state matching.

The School Breakfast Program
The School Breakfast Program provides federal funds to assist in providing breakfasts to children in schools and residential child care institutions. Like the School Lunch Program, the program must operate on a nonprofit basis and provide meals that meet the nutritional criteria set by the U.S. Department of Agriculture.

All children who attend a participating school may receive subsidized breakfasts. Children are charged for each meal according to the family income. Children from families with incomes at or below 130 percent of the federal poverty income level are eligible for free breakfast; those from families with incomes above 130 percent but at or below 185 percent of the poverty level are eligible for reduced-price breakfast; and children from families with incomes above 185 percent of poverty are eligible for breakfast at the full price.

Eligible Schools. All public elementary and secondary schools are eligible to participate in the school breakfast program. Private, nonprofit elementary and secondary schools and public and private, nonprofit licensed resi-

Table 31. Selected Statistics on the Food Stamp Program

Fiscal Year	(in billions of dollars) Total Federal Spending	(in millions of persons) Average Monthly Participation
1988	$13.3	20.1
1989	$13.8	20.2
1990	$16.5	21.5
1991 (est.)	$19.8	24.1
1992	$23.5	26.9
1993	$28.1	Not Available

dential child care institutions also are eligible to participate.

Administration. The program is administered at the federal level by the Food and Nutrition Service of the U.S. Department of Agriculture and by state educational agencies (SEAs) at the state level.

Federal Funding. SEAs reimburse participating schools with federal assistance according to reimbursement rates set by statute and adjusted for inflation each July 1, and based on the number of breakfasts served. The amount of federal reimbursement varies according to the family income of each participating child. An established reimbursement rate is available to all participating schools and institutions for breakfasts served to nonpoor children. Higher rates are set for breakfasts that are served free or at a reduced price to low-income children. Schools that serve more than 40 percent of their school lunches to lower-income children also may receive "severe need" reimbursement for breakfasts. Schools are free to set fees for full-price breakfasts for nonpoor children. Schools may set prices for full-price breakfasts that are higher than their costs to assist them in meeting uncovered costs for free and reduced-price breakfasts. Schools, however, may not make an overall profit on their breakfast programs.

State Match. There are no state matching requirements for federal funds provided to the school breakfast program.

The Surplus Food Program

The surplus food program, administered by the Food and Nutrition Service of the U.S. Department of Agriculture, is designed to benefit low-income persons, welfare recipients, and the unemployed through direct provision of commodities.

The food, donated via USDA surplus removal and price support programs, is distributed to a variety of public and nonprofit institutions designated by individual states. The state food commodity distribution agency should be contacted for information on service agency eligibility. Children in schools and child care institutions are among those eligible under federal guidelines to benefit from the surplus food donation program.

The Surplus Food Program: A Summary

Nature of Program
Provides surplus food from other USDA programs for distribution to public and nonprofit institutions serving low-income persons, welfare recipients, and the unemployed.

Funding Type
Commodity distribution.

For More Information
Deputy Administrator, Food Stamp Program, Food and Nutrition Services, U.S. Department of Agriculture, Alexandria, VA 22302. Phone: 703/756–3022.

Chapter 11
Funding for Health, Mental Health, and Substance Abuse Services

There are many sources of federal funding for health, mental health, and substance abuse services. Among those most relevant to financing services for vulnerable children, young people, and families are the Maternal and Child Health Block Grant (Title V of the Social Security Act); the Family Planning Program (Title X of the Public Health Service Act); the Substance Abuse and the Mental Health Services Block Grants; the Substance Abuse Discretionary Grants, and a new funding source, the Children of Substance Abusers (COSA) program. In addition, the Ryan White Care Act specifically targets services for individuals affected by AIDS and HIV infection.

Title V: The Maternal and Child Health Block Grant

The Maternal and Child Health (MCH) Block Grant enables states to develop, maintain, and strengthen the planning, coordination, delivery, and evaluation of health care for mothers and children, particularly those with inadequate access to health care. The MCH Block Grant consolidates seven previous formula and categorical grant programs:

1. The Maternal and Child Health and Crippled Children's Program.

2. The program of supportive services for children with disabilities who receive SSI.

3. Hemophilia treatment.

4. Lead-based paint poisoning prevention.

5. The Sudden Infant Death Syndrome (SIDS) program.

6. Genetic screening and counseling.

7. Adolescent pregnancy services.

Funding

Each year, 85 percent of the funding appropriated for the MCH Block Grant is allocated among the states; the remaining 15 percent is retained by the U.S. Department of Health and Human Services for its Special Projects of Regional and National Significance (SPRANS) grants. In each state, 30 percent of MCH Block Grant funds are earmarked for services to children with special health care needs, 30 percent are for preventive and primary care services, and 40 percent are left to state discretion.

For FY 1993, $664.64 million was appropriated for the MCH Block Grant; for FY 1994, $792 million was appropriated. Federal law provides that when funding for the Block Grant in any fiscal year exceeds $600 million, a set-aside is mandated for a variety of federally administered demonstration projects. This set-aside is set at 12.75 percent of the amount over $600 million. For FY 1994, funding for these special projects was made available at 12.75 percent of $192 million (the difference between the $792 million appropriation and the $600 million amount that triggers the set-aside). These funds have been used for such projects as maternal and infant home visiting, efforts to increase provider participation in MCH programs, integrated service delivery or "one-stop shopping" services, nonprofit hospital-MCH centers, rural maternal and child health care programs, and community

Title V: The Maternal and Child Health Block Grant: A Summary

Nature of Program
Provides funds to states for maternal and child health services. Funds may be used for primary care services for children; immunizations; preventive care; prenatal, delivery, and postpartum services; and rehabilitation services for children with disabilities. Individual eligibility is established by each state. In most cases, women and children who are eligible for Medicaid are also eligible for Maternal and Child Health (MCH) services.

Funding Type
Block grant. States must contribute $3 in nonfederal funds for each $4 of MCH funds.

For More Information
Maternal and Child Health Bureau, HRSA-PHA-DHHS, 5600 Fishers Lane, Room 9-11, Rockville, MD 20857. Phone: 301/443–3163.

projects for children with special health care needs.

Services
The MCH Block Grant funds services to prevent disabling conditions among children; immunization programs; primary care services for children; prenatal, delivery, and postpartum services for low-income mothers; and rehabilitative services for children who are disabled and receive SSI.

Grantees
Grantees under the MCH Block Grant are primarily state health departments. In many states, however, state health departments subcontract with local or regional health departments, migrant worker and community health centers, and private providers to deliver maternal and child health care services.

Eligibility
MCH eligibility criteria are established by each state. In most states, women and children who are eligible for Medicaid are also eligible for MCH services.

Federal Match
For each $4 of federal funds under the MCH Block Grant, a state must contribute $3 in nonfederal funds.

Title X: Family Planning Services
Title X of the Public Health Service Act provides support for family planning clinics, training of family planning personnel, and the development and dissemination of family planning and population growth information to all persons who seek the information.

Family Planning Clinics
The Office of Family Planning within the U.S. Department of Health and Human Services directly awards most funds under Title X to facilities that qualify as family planning clinics. In FY 1989, 4,000 clinics received some form of Title X support.

Participating clinics are required to offer a broad range of services considered to be "acceptable and effective," including natural family planning

Family Planning Services (Title X of the Public Health Service Act): A Summary

Nature of Program
Provides funding for family planning services. Grants are awarded directly to public or nonprofit entities that qualify as family planning clinics.

Funding Type
Yearly appropriation. There is no specific state match requirement; however, no clinic may be supported solely by Title X funds.

For More Information
Office of Family Planning, PHS-DHHS, Hubert H. Humphrey Building, Room 736E, 200 Independence Avenue, SW, Washington, DC 20201. Phone: 202/619–0257.

methods, nondirective counseling services, physical examinations (including cancer detection and laboratory tests), infertility services, pregnancy tests, contraceptive supplies, periodic follow-up examinations, referral to and from other social and medical service agencies, and supportive services.

Eligibility
Federal law does not mandate a target population for Title X services. Federal regulations, however, require that priority in the provision of family planning clinic services be given to persons from low-income families. Clinics must provide services free of charge to persons whose income is at or below 100 percent of the federal poverty level.

Funding
Congress appropriated $150 million for the Title X family planning program for FY 1992, a small increase (four percent) in funding over the previous year. Funding was significantly increased for FY 1993 to $173.6 million and to $180.9 million for FY 1994. Funding is distributed through grants and contracts to public and nonprofit private entities to establish and operate family planning clinics. The Office of Family Planning in the U.S. Department of Health and Human Services allocates funds to regional offices, which in turn determine which family planning projects will be funded. No specific state matching requirements exist for these grants. Federal regulations, however, provide that no family planning clinic project grant may be supported solely by Title X funds.

The Substance Abuse and Mental Health Services Block Grants

The Alcohol, Drug Abuse, and Mental Health Services (ADMS) Block Grant, previously administered by the Alcohol, Drug Abuse, and Mental Health Administration (ADAMHA) of the Pub-

Substance Abuse and Mental Health Services Block Grants: A Summary

Nature of Program
Provides funding to states through two block grants: one for mental health services and one for substance abuse prevention and treatment services.
Funding Type
Yearly appropriation.
For More Information
Public Health Advisor, Office for Treatment Improvement, SAMSHA - PHS-DHHS, Rockwall II Building, 10th Floor, 5600 Fishers Lane, Rockville, MD 20857.
Phone: 301/443–3820.

lic Health Service of the U.S. Department of Health and Human Services, had long been the primary source of federal funding to assist states in developing and providing mental health and substance abuse prevention and treatment services. Under the 1992 Alcohol, Drug Abuse and Mental Health Reorganization Act (P.L. 102-321), the ADMS Block Grant, which originally funded both mental health and substance abuse services, was split into two block grants, one for alcohol and drug abuse treatment services and the other for community mental health services. Beginning in FY 1993, states received two separate appropriations—one for substance abuse services and one for mental health services. In FY 1993 and FY 1994, states were permitted, however, to continue to transfer funds between the two block grants.

The Substance Abuse Block Grant was funded at $1.1 billion in FY 1993 and at $1.167 billion in FY 1994; the Mental Health Block Grant was funded at $277.9 million in FY 1993 and at the same level in FY 1994. The formula for distributing the funds takes into account such factors as population and relative per capita income, as did the formula under the prior legislation. Under the new legislation, however, the formula places less weight on urban factors in order to better acknowledge the needs of rural areas and smaller states.

Changes in the Block Grant were accompanied by a reorganization of ADAMHA. There is no longer an administrative entity called ADAMHA; instead, there are two administrative entities: the National Institutes of Health (NIH), which oversees all research; and the Substance Abuse and Mental Health Services Administration (SAMHSA), which oversees all service delivery. Table 32 outlines this administrative structure.

The Substance Abuse Block Grant

The Substance Abuse Block Grant funds alcohol and drug abuse prevention, treatment, and aftercare services. States are required under the block grant to give pregnant women and intravenous drug users preference in admission to treatment programs and to make interim services available while individuals in these groups await admission to treatment programs. When a state cannot provide immediate treatment services for intravenous drug users, it must provide interim services within 48 hours and assure that the individual is admitted to comprehensive treatment within 120 days. For FY 1993 and FY 1994, there is a set-aside of five percent to increase services to pregnant women and women with dependent children. Facilities that receive funds under the set-aside and provide residential or outpatient substance abuse treatment must also provide prenatal health care and child day care services. Several other provisions also govern the operation of the Substance Abuse Block Grant:

1. Any agency receiving Substance Abuse Block Grant funds must make tuberculosis services available. Block grant funds may be used for tuberculosis services.

2. States with a rate of Acquired Immune Deficiency Syndrome

(AIDS) equal to 10 per 100,000 individuals must set aside a proportion of their Substance Abuse Block Grant funds for nonhospital early-intervention HIV services at substance abuse treatment sites. The proportion ranges from two to five percent. Twenty states, the District of Columbia, and Puerto Rico are currently affected by this provision.

3. As a condition of receiving block grant funds in FY 1994 and FY 1995, each state must enforce laws prohibiting the sale or distribution of tobacco products to children below age 18. Failure to do so will trigger the loss of a percentage of block grant funds.

The Mental Health Block Grant

The Mental Health Block Grant is designed to support the development of community mental health ser-

vices. Under the prior ADMS Block Grant, 10 percent of each state's mental health funding was set aside for children's mental health services. The new legislation retained that 10-percent set-aside, but added another 10 percent increase for FY 1993, and yet another 10 percent in FY 1994. As a result, by the end of FY 1994, 30 percent of a state's mental health allotment must be devoted to programs for children.

States now must meet two new administrative requirements to receive mental health funds. First, each state must submit a plan that identifies how community mental health services will be provided to adults and children with serious emotional disturbance. Second, each state must establish a state mental health planning council.

In addition, P.L. 102-321 expands the list of eligible providers of mental

Table 32. P.L. 102-321: The Reorganization of the Alcohol, Drug Abuse and Mental Health Administration

National Institutes of Health (NIH)	Substance Abuse and Mental Health Services Administration (SAMHSA)
National Institute of Mental Health (NIMH)	Center for Substance Abuse Prevention (CSAP) ■ Administers programs previously administered by the Office of Substance Abuse Prevention (OSAP)
National Institute on Drug Abuse (NIDA)	Center for Mental Health Services (CMHS) ■ Coordinates all mental health activities under the mental health block grant ■ Administers the new Childhood Mental Health Program
National Institute on Alcohol Abuse and Alcoholism (NIAAA)	Center for Substance Abuse Treatment (CSAT) ■ Administers the Substance Abuse Block Grant ■ Administers the pregnant and postpartum women's programs

health services. Under the prior legislation, all federal mental health funds had to be "passed through" to community mental health centers (CMHC). Under P.L. 102-321, however, "qualified community programs" may now receive direct financial support from the state agency that administers the Mental Health Block Grant. "Qualified community programs" include not only the CMHCs, but also child welfare agencies, child mental health programs, and psychosocial rehabilitation programs.

It should be noted that P.L. 102-321, in addition to redesigning the block grant, created the Comprehensive Community Mental Health Services for Children with Serious Emotional Disturbances program. The program is designed to support multiagency, community-based approaches to mental health services for children.

Upon receiving federal funds, public entities, including states and localities, are required to collaborate with child-serving agencies, including child welfare, mental health, education, and juvenile justice agencies, in implementing a comprehensive system of care. Agencies receiving funds under the program must provide diagnosis and evaluation, outpatient services, emergency care, intensive home-based services, intensive day treatment, respite care, transition services, therapeutic foster care and family foster care, and group care in facilities that care for no more than 10 children. Child welfare agencies with more than 10 beds may participate if they agree to provide services on "an

ambulatory or outpatient basis." Each child served under the program must have a plan of care that outlines the responsibilities of each agency that participates in the system of care. Eligibility for services extends to all children under the age of 21 and their families, include biological, adoptive, and foster parents.

Substance Abuse Discretionary Grants

The Centers for Substance Abuse Prevention and Substance Abuse Treatment of the Public Health Service of the U.S. Department of Health and Human Services administer several competitive grant programs designed to serve substance-involved women, children, and youths. Three of the programs are particularly relevant to financing services for substance involved children, youths, and pregnant and postpartum women.

Prevention Demonstration Grants Targeting High-Risk Youths

These grants fund alcohol and drug abuse prevention activities that target youths at risk of developing substance abuse problems. The Anti-Drug Abuse Act of 1988 broadened the category of high-risk youths to be served under this program to include abused and/or neglected youths, homeless or runaway youths, youths with physical or mental disabilities, pregnant teenagers, school dropouts, children of abusers of alcohol and other drugs, latchkey children, and economically disadvantaged youths. Demonstration grants are awarded to community-based programs that develop and evaluate approaches specifically designed to decrease the prevalence of alcohol and other drug problems among high-risk youths, increase the resiliency of high-risk youths, coordinate community activities aimed at preventing alcohol and other drug problems among youths, and increase the access of high-risk youths to treatment and rehabilitation services. The program was funded at $56.3 million for FY 1993 and at $63.3 million for FY 1994.

Model Projects for Pregnant and Postpartum Women and Their Infants

These demonstration grant projects focus on prevention, education, and treatment activities for pregnant and postpartum women who are substance involved. Successful projects have included promising models and innovative approaches to prevent or minimize fetal exposure to alcohol and other drugs and projects that coordinate existing community services with new or expanded services. Many of these programs focus on the development of an array of therapeutic programs and the integration of comprehensive supportive services that include health care and educational services, voluntary organizations, and other relevant community-based agencies and service systems.

P.L. 102-321 outlined two distinct targets for this program. One target is long-term residential treatment services for pregnant and postpartum women and their children; the second is outpatient treatment programs. For FY 1994, the total appropriation for both programs was $49.2 million, with priority to be given to the residential program. The residential program may also receive additional funds from the special Asset Forfeiture Fund administered by the Treasury Department and from the SAMHSA

Substance Abuse Discretionary Grants: A Summary

Nature of Program
Provides funding through competitive grants for programs that serve children, youths, and pregnant and postpartum women. Eligible projects include: prevention programs targeting high-risk youths; model projects for pregnant women and their infants; and community partnership programs involving local agencies and providers.

Funding Type
Yearly appropriation.

For More Information
Center for Substance Abuse Prevention and Center for Substance Abuse Treatment, SAMSHA-PHS-DHHS, Rockwall II Building, 5600 Fishers Lane, Rockville, MD 20857. Phone: 301/443-3958.

Technical Assistance, Data Collection and Evaluation account.

Programs providing residential treatment under this SAMHSA program must provide certain services: an individualized treatment plan; individual, group, and family counseling; aftercare services; prenatal and postpartum health care; referrals for hospital services as needed; parenting training; HIV counseling; sexual abuse and domestic violence counseling; employment counseling; child care; and family preservation counseling. Providers of outpatient services must offer prevention and treatment services to pregnant and postpartum women and outpatient treatment for children who have been affected by their mothers' substance abuse.

The Community Partnership Grants Program

This program addresses alcohol and other drug problems through community-based coalitions of public agencies and private organizations. The initiative supports an estimated 150

demonstration grants, each funded at $100,000 to $500,000, with financial support for up to five years. Projects develop comprehensive, self-sustaining, and replicable systems within communities, involving health, education, law enforcement, social services, grassroots community, and religious organizations in the prevention of and intervention into alcohol and other drug abuse. Grantees are required to demonstrate effective training, evaluation, and capacity-building strategies.

The Children of Substance Abusers Program

Authorized by the Alcohol, Drug Abuse and Mental Health Reorganization Act of 1991 (P.L 102-321), the Children of Substance Abusers (COSA) Program provides funding for comprehensive services to children and families affected by parental substance abuse. The program supports a broad range of services provided through

The Children of Substance Abusers (COSA) Program: A Summary

Nature of the Program
Provides funding for a comprehensive range of services to children and families affected by substance abuse and services to caregivers of substance-affected children. Also funds home visiting programs.
Funding Type
Yearly appropriation.
For More Information
Health Resources and Services Administration, Department of Health and Human Services, Public Health Service, 5600 Fishers Lane, Room 9-48, Rockville, MD 20857. Phone: 301/443-9051.

comprehensive, community-based service systems. Eligibility is very broad, extending to children cared for by biological parents, relatives, foster parents, or adoptive parents. Services are to be made available to children affected in any way by parental substance abuse, and the children are eligible irrespective of parental participation in the program. The program is not limited to infants exposed prenatally to drugs.

COSA has two components—a direct service grant program and a home visiting program. Both of these initiatives will be administered by the Health Resources and Services Administration (HRSA) of the Public Health Service. P.L. 102-321, however, requires that HRSA consult with the Administration for Children, Youth and Families (ACYF) concerning program guidelines.

Although $50 million has been authorized for both FY 1993 and FY 1994 to address the service needs of pregnant women, caregiver parents, infants, and young children, the program is yet to be funded. The major provisions of COSA are as follows:

Consortium Grants

These grants fund one grantee or several grantees who will be responsible for coordinating the participation of multiple service agencies, including health, mental health, child welfare, juvenile justice, and substance abuse treatment programs. Not only are child welfare agencies specifically listed as eligible grantees, but the law requires that every grantee establish "a collaborative relationship with child welfare agencies and child protective

services that will enable the applicant to—(i) advocate for children...in child protective services cases, (ii) provide services to help prevent the unnecessary placement of children in substitute care, and (iii) promote reunification of families."

Services. There are three categories of individuals for whom services may be provided. For children, eligible services include periodic medical and developmental evaluations, primary pediatric care, therapeutic intervention services, and preventive counseling services. For families, eligible services include counseling and assistance in obtaining treatment for substance abuse. For substance abusers and their caregivers, eligible services include family assessments, therapeutic intervention services, and child care and parent skills training.

Personnel Preparation. Fifteen percent of all COSA funding above $25 million is earmarked for training, including training for "child welfare personnel."

Home Visiting

The second major component of COSA is the home visiting program. In developing the home visiting program authorized by COSA, HRSA must consult with ACYF, and with the National Commission to Prevent Infant Mortality (NCPIM) .

Eligibility. Under the Home Visiting program, the term *eligible family*, means either a pregnant woman at risk of delivering an infant with a health or developmental complication or a child below the age of three who: (1) has experienced or is at risk of a health or developmental complication, (2) has experienced child abuse and neglect, or (3) has been prenatally exposed to alcohol or other drugs through maternal substance abuse. For eligibility purposes, a woman is considered "at risk of delivering a child with a health or developmental complication" if during the pregnancy she lacks access to routine prenatal care, lacks transportation, lacks child care, is fearful of accessing substance abuse services, or is a low-income minor.

Services. P.L. 102-321 requires the following services to be available (either directly or through arrangement) under the home visiting program: prenatal and postnatal health care, primary health care for children, parenting education, and assistance in obtaining access to health, mental health, developmental, social, housing, and nutrition services. The programs are expected to specifically facilitate access to Medicaid, the Supplemental Food Program for Women, Infants and Children (WIC), the Supplemental Security Income (SSI) program, and substance abuse treatment.

Case Management Model. Home visiting services are to be delivered using a case management model, with a registered nurse or social worker assigned as the case manager. This individual is responsible for the development of a family service plan containing an assessment of family needs and a structured plan for service delivery.

Home Visiting Team. Without specifying who will actually conduct home visits, P.L. 102-321 requires that the home visiting team include, as appropriate, nurses, social workers, child welfare professionals, infant and early childhood specialists, nutritionists, and lay persons trained as home visitors. A related provision requires that when HRSA makes individual grant awards, it must consider "different combinations of professional and lay home visitors utilized within programs that are reflective of the identified service needs and characteristics of target populations."

Peer Review. P.L. 102-321 requires all home visiting grants be examined by a peer review panel composed of national experts in the fields of maternal and child health and child abuse and neglect and representatives from SAMHSA, ACYF, the National Commission to Prevent Infant Mortality (NCPIM), and the U.S. Advisory Board on Child Abuse and Neglect.

Eligible Entities. Entities eligible for funding include community health centers, hospitals, local health departments, family service agencies, child welfare agencies, family resource and support programs, developmental disabilities service providers, and resource mother projects.

Federal Responses to HIV Infection and AIDS: The Ryan White CARE Act

The Ryan White Comprehensive AIDS Resources Emergency (CARE) Act is a major source of funding for services to individuals with HIV infection or AIDS. In FY 1993, the appropriation was $348.2 million and in FY 1994, $579.4 million.

The Ryan White CARE Act funds four major types of programs:

1. Title I of the Act provides, under a funding formula, emergency assistance to cities that are experiencing the highest rates of HIV infection and AIDS.

2. Title II of the Act funds the HIV CARE Grant Program. Funds under Title II are directed to state health departments (90 percent of Title II funds) and to special projects of national significance (10 percent of Title II funds) that are conducted by public and private nonprofit entities. The grant awards under Title II support consortia that provide a comprehensive array of services to individuals and families affected by HIV. Emphasis is on home- and community-based care, including mental health, developmental, and rehabilitative services. Under Title II, 15 percent of funds must be set aside for services to women, infants, children, adolescents, and families affected by HIV. The special projects of national significance have included programs focusing on access to care, advocacy services, and integration of mental and physical health services.

3. Title III-B of the Act funds early intervention services through state formula grants and competitive categorical grants. Eligible grantees for the categorical grants include private nonprofit entities that provide comprehensive primary care services to populations at risk for HIV infection.

4. Title IV of the Act includes the Pediatric and Adolescent AIDS Demonstration Projects. The purpose of the grants under this program is to support the development of an infrastructure to provide family-centered, community-based, coordinated and culturally competent services for HIV-infected

The Ryan White CARE Act: A Summary

Nature of Program
The Ryan White Act funds a range of services for adults and children affected by HIV and AIDS, including home- and community-based services with mental health and developmental components. Included within the Act are the Pediatric and Adolescent AIDS Demonstration Projects, which support the development of models to prevent and treat HIV infection in women and children.

Funding Type
Yearly appropriation.

For More Information
Division of HIV Services, Bureau of Health Resources Development, HRSA-PHS-DHHS, 5600 Fishers Lane, Room 9A-05, Rockville, MD 20857. Phone: 301/443–0652.

children and young people and their families. Historically, projects have funded strategies and innovative models that prevent HIV infection, particularly through reduction of perinatal transmission, and that provide coordinated treatment, support, and social services for children, youths, and women of childbearing age who are HIV infected. Emphasis has been on outpatient services that use a case management approach. Eligible entities include public, nonprofit, and for-profit, private entities. In FY 1993, $20.9 million was appropriated. In FY 1994, when the program became a part of Title IV of the Act, it received $22 million in appropriations.

Chapter 12
Federal Funding for Juvenile Justice Services

Federal funding for juvenile justice programs is available through three major sources: the Juvenile Justice and Delinquency Prevention Act, the Runaway and Homeless Youth Act, and the Anti-Drug Abuse Act of 1988.

The Juvenile Justice and Delinquency Prevention Act

The Office of Juvenile Justice and Delinquency Prevention (OJJDP) in the U.S. Department of Justice is the primary federal agency addressing juvenile justice and related issues. Established by Congress in 1974 through the Juvenile Justice and Delinquency Prevention (JJDP) Act, OJJDP promotes state and local solutions to problems confronting youths in the juvenile justice system. The OJJDP Administrator oversees funding activities authorized by Title II of the JJDP Act, including state formula grants, special emphasis programs, programs to prevent juvenile gangs and drug trafficking, missing children's assistance programs, and a variety of specifically targeted efforts. Table 33 sets forth the recent funding history for these programs.

State Formula Grants
The State Formula Grants program is designed to increase the capacity of state and local governments to develop effective education, training,

research, prevention, diversion, treatment, and rehabilitation programs in the area of juvenile delinquency and to develop effective programs within the juvenile justice system. Legislation reauthorizing the Juvenile Justice and Delinquency Prevention Act of 1992 placed increased emphasis on this grant program, mandating that states utilize funds to (1) remove status offenders from secure facilities, (2) remove juveniles from adult jails, and (3) make efforts to address minority overrepresentation in the juvenile justice system.

Funding and Allocation. Formula grant funds are allocated to states and territories on the basis of their relative population under age 18. A minimum of $325,000 is allocated to each

Juvenile Justice and Delinquency Prevention Act Programs: A Summary

Nature of Programs

1. *State Formula Grants:* Block grants to states for juvenile justice programs, including education, prevention, treatment, and diversion programs. At least two-thirds of the grant must be passed through to programs or local governments for law enforcement.

2. *Special Emphasis Program:* Discretionary grants to design and demonstrate innovative approaches to preventing and controlling juvenile delinquency. Examples of projects include community-based alternatives to institutional confinement, advocacy for youths in the juvenile justice system, and family strengthening activities.

3. *Discretionary Grants:* Grants to fund programs aimed at reducing juvenile involvement in gang-related activities and drug abuse and trafficking.

4. *Missing Children's Assistance Programs:* Funds national clearinghouse and resource center on missing children.

Funding Type

1. *State Formula Grants:* Yearly appropriation. Funds used for planning require a 50 percent state match. No match is needed for service delivery programs.

2. *Special Emphasis Programs:* Yearly appropriation. Cash match not required except for construction projects.

3. *Juvenile Gangs and Drug Abuse and Drug Trafficking Programs:* Yearly appropriation. Cash match not required.

4. *Missing Children's Assistance Programs:* Yearly appropriation.

For More Information

Office of Juvenile Justice and Delinquency Prevention, U.S. Department of Justice, Washington, DC 20531. Phone: 202/307–5921.

state and $75,000 to each territory. If at any time the appropriation for Title II programs equals or exceeds $75 million (excluding Part D of the Act, which provides funds for "Prevention and Treatment Programs Relating to Juvenile Gangs and Drug Abuse and Drug Trafficking"), the minimum allocation for each state increases to $400,000 per state and $100,000 per territory. At least two-thirds of the funds received by the state must be "expended by" or "passed through to" programs or units of local government, private nonprofit agencies, and Native American tribes that perform law enforcement functions.

Implementation. The chief executive of each state applying for a formula grant must establish or designate a state agency to supervise the preparation and administration of the plan for services under this program. Individual projects within states receive funding at the discretion of the designated state agency.

Federal and State Match. When state formula grant funds are used for planning, the state must match each federal dollar with a nonfederal dollar. No match is required when federal funds under this program are used for service delivery programs.

Services. Projects funded through the State Formula Grants program offer a wide range of services, including community-based services for the prevention and treatment of juvenile delinquency, the establishment of group homes and halfway houses, screening and intake services to permit increased diversion from juvenile court processes, expanded use of probation, enhanced training for personnel who work in the juvenile delinquency field, and activities to remove status offenders from secure detention, separate juveniles from contact with incarcerated adults, and remove juveniles from adult jails or lockups.

Special Emphasis Programs

Special Emphasis programs develop and implement projects that design, test, and demonstrate effective approaches, techniques, and methods for preventing and controlling juvenile delinquency. Examples of projects funded under this program include:

- community-based alternatives to institutional confinement;

Table 33. Programs Under the Juvenile Justice and Delinquency Prevention Act: Recent Funding History

Program	(in millions of dollars)		
	FY 1992	FY 1993	FY 1994
■ Juvenile Justice and Delinquency Prevention State Formula Grants	$50.80	$51.10	$59.50
■ Special Emphasis	$18.10	$18.30	$21.30
■ Juvenile Gang and Drug Trafficking	$3.50	$4.00	$5.00
■ Missing Children's Assistance	$8.50	$8.47	$14.50

- the development and implementation of effective means of diverting juveniles from the traditional juvenile justice and correctional system;
- programs that stress advocacy activities aimed at improving services to youths in the juvenile justice system;
- model programs to strengthen and maintain the family unit;
- prevention and treatment programs for juveniles who commit serious crimes; and
- a national law-related education program of delinquency prevention.

Special Emphasis funds are available to public and private nonprofit agencies, organizations, individuals, state and local units of government, and combinations of state and local units. These grants do not require a cash match, with the exception of construction projects for which the nonfederal match is 50 percent.

Juvenile Gangs and Drug Trafficking Program

This program supports programs and activities involving families and communities that are designed to accomplish the following:

- Reduce the participation of juveniles, particularly youngsters in elementary and secondary schools, in drug-related crimes.
- Develop within the juvenile adjudicatory and correctional systems new and innovative means to address the problems of juveniles convicted of serious drug-related and gang-related offenses.
- Reduce juvenile involvement in gang-related activities, particularly activities that involve the distribution of drugs by or to juveniles.
- Promote the involvement of juveniles in lawful activities in areas in which gangs commit crimes.
- Provide treatment to juveniles who are members of gangs, including members who are accused of committing a serious crime and members who have been adjudicated as being delinquent.
- Support activities to inform juveniles of the availability of treatment and services for which financial assistance is provided under the program.
- Facilitate federal and state cooperation with local school officials to assist juveniles who are likely to participate in gang activities.
- Facilitate coordination and cooperation among local education, juvenile justice, employment, and social services agencies to prevent or reduce the participation of juveniles in gang activities.
- Provide personnel, personnel training, equipment, and supplies in conjunction with programs and activities designed to prevent or reduce the participation of juveniles in unlawful gang activities or unlawful drug activities and to assist in improving the adjudicative and correctional components of the juvenile justice system.
- Provide pre- and post-trial drug abuse treatment to youngsters in the juvenile justice system.
- Provide drug abuse education, prevention, and treatment involving police and juvenile officials in demand reduction programs.

The 1992 reauthorizing legislation for the JJDP Act strengthened this program by creating two new discretionary programs: Gang-Free Schools and Communities, and Community-Based Gang Intervention.

Projects funded during FY 1990 included programs to prevent high school students from dropping out of school and joining gangs, programs aimed at reducing teen victimization, and programs to provide training and technical assistance to key policymakers in order to improve public and private efforts to prevent, intervene in, and suppress drug and gang activities.

Funds for all projects, including those created by the 1992 legislation, are available to public or private nonprofit agencies or organizations and individuals. No state or local match is required.

Missing Children's Assistance Program

This program provides funds to ensure effective coordination among all federally funded programs involved in locating and serving missing children. Funds are to be used to

1. Establish and maintain a national resource center and clearinghouse to:
   - provide technical assistance to local and state governments, public and private nonprofit agencies, and individuals in finding missing children;
   - coordinate public and private programs to locate and recover missing children;
   - disseminate nationally information on innovative missing children's programs, services, and legislation; and
   - provide technical assistance to law enforcement agencies, private nonprofit agencies, and individuals involved in the prevention, investigation, prosecution, and treatment of cases involving missing or exploited children.

2. Periodically conduct national incidence studies to determine the actual number of children reported missing each year, the number of children who are victims of stranger abductions, the number of children who are victims of parental kidnappings, and the number of missing children who are recovered each year.

3. Compile, analyze, publish, and disseminate an annual summary of research on missing children, to include an annual comprehensive plan for assuring cooperation and coordination among all agencies and organizations with responsibilities for missing children.

4. Provide a program to establish and maintain a national 24-hour toll-free telephone number through which individuals may report information regarding missing children.

Funds are available to public and private nonprofit agencies, organizations, individuals, state and local units of government, and combinations of state and local units. State and local matching funds are not required.

Special Initiatives

In addition to the programs described above, OJJDP has developed a number of special initiatives. Table 34 summarizes information about selected OJJDP initiatives.

Table 34. OJJDP Special Initiatives

Initiative	Purpose
Boot Camps for Juvenile Offenders	Designed to serve as a criminal sanction; promote strong ethical and moral values such as honesty, personal integrity, positive self-image, and self-responsibility; increase academic achievement; provide discipline through physical conditioning and teamwork; incorporate activities and resources to reduce drug and alcohol abuse among juvenile offenders; encourage participants to become productive law-abiding citizens; promote literacy by using intensive, systematic phonics; and instill a work ethic among juvenile offenders.
Teens, Crime and the Community: Teens in Action in the 1990s	Designed to reduce teen victimization by actively engaging teens in helping to improve their schools.
Targeted Outreach with a Gang Prevention and Intervention Component	Designed to support the efforts of local Boys and Girls Clubs to prevent youths from entering gangs and to intervene with gang members early in their careers in an effort to divert them from gang activity.
Family Strengthening Program	Designed to develop and support programs that strengthen and maintain families as a way of preventing or treating juvenile delinquency.
National Juvenile Firesetter/Arson Control and Prevention Program	Designed to develop models and provide training and technical assistance to communities to prevent juvenile firesetting and arson.
Partnership Plan, Phase V	Developed as a national school dropout prevention model that is being implemented by Cites in Schools, Inc. (CIS). CIS provides training and technical assistance to states and local communities to enable them to adapt and implement the CIS dropout prevention model. The model focuses on social issues, employment, mental health issues, and community resources as they relate to high-risk youths and their families at the school level.
Anti-Drug Abuse Prevention—Technical Assistance Voucher Project	Designed to provide technical assistance to neighborhood-based organizations that have established antidrug abuse projects to enhance their capacity to serve high-risk youths and serious juvenile offenders.
Reaching At-Risk Youths in Public Housing Program	To support activities of the Boys and Girls Clubs of America to establish seven Boys and Girls Clubs in public housing across the country under the existing cooperative agreement with OJJDP. These programs are designed to provide services to high-risk youths who live in public housing in an attempt to prevent involvement in delinquency, drug and alcohol abuse, and gang activity.
Promising Approaches for the Prevention, Intervention in, and Treatment of Illegal Drug and Alcohol Use among Juveniles	Designed to provide communities with skills and information to adopt and implement promising approaches for preventing, intervening in, and treating chronic juvenile drug and alcohol abuse.

OJJDP has implemented three boot camp sites: Boys and Girls Club of Greater Mobile, Mobile, AL; Cuyahoga County Juvenile Court, Cleveland, OH; and Colorado Division of Youth Services, Denver, CO.

Activities include training, technical assistance, program replication, and dissemination of materials to significantly increase the capacity of schools and other institutions to prevent juvenile victimization.

The National Office of Boys and Girls Clubs provides training and technical assistance to local clubs to help them prevent juveniles from entering gangs and to help them develop the capacity to intervene with gang youths.

The program utilizes research to analyze how families function effectively, including parent-child dynamics, nurturing, and family-community involvement, particularly as those factors relate to delinquency prevention.

In the first phase of the program, an assessment report, a policies and procedures manual, and a training curriculum were developed. Four sites are implementing the model program. Training, technical assistance, and evaluation are major activities.

Individualized plans have been developed by CIS for each youngster in existing programs. Remedial education, social services and other supports are provided to youth and their families. CIS is committed to establishing a traditional CIS program in at least one school within the target neighborhoods in each of ten Weed and Seed sites where CIS has implemented a program network.

Neighborhood groups have applied for and received vouchers, ranging in amount from $1000 to $10,000, depending on community needs. Groups present individualized plans for the requested technical assistance. The program is being implemented by the National Center for Neighborhood Enterprise.

Funds have been used to establish sites and provide training and technical assistance to Boys and Girls Clubs and public housing authorities who wish to establish clubs.

Funding has been used to complete an assessment of promising prevention, intervention and treatment, and aftercare programs and an evaluation of all the components of the community-based models and the related training and technical assistance.

In FY 1992, OJJDP made programs for gangs and violent offenders its top priority. In FY 1993, emphasis was placed on reducing serious, violent, and chronic crime through a range of prevention, intervention, and secure confinement sanctions and treatment strategies. Table 35 presents some of OJJDP's FY 1992 and FY 1993 discretionary program plans.

The Runaway and Homeless Youth Act

The Runaway and Homeless Youth Act funds tow major programs: the Runaway and Homeless Youth Act Program and the Transitional Living for Runaway and Homeless Youth Program.

The Runaway and Homeless Youth Program

The Administration for Children, Youth and Families (ACYF) of the U.S. Department of Health and Human Services administers the Runaway and Homeless Youth Program to develop local facilities to address the immediate needs of runaway and homeless youths and their families. Project funds are used to:

- Establish and operate local centers that provide services to meet the immediate needs of runaway and homeless youths and their families for temporary shelter, food, and related services without the involvement of law enforcement or the juvenile justice system.

- Establish and operate a toll-free national communications system to assist runaway and homeless youths in communicating with their families and service providers.

- Provide technical assistance and training.

Runaway and Homeless Youth Act Programs: A Summary

Nature of Programs

1. *The Runaway and Homeless Youth Program:* Funds local facilities, including youth centers and a tollfree telephone line, to address the immediate needs of runaway and homeless youths and their families.

2. *The Transitional Living for Runaway and Homeless Youth Program:* Funds local programs that assist homeless youths in making the transition to adulthood and self-sufficiency.

Funding Type

Yearly appropriation for each program. The Transitional Living for Runaway and Homeless Youth Program requires a 10 percent nonfederal match.

For More Information

Family and Youth Services Bureau, Administration for Children, Youth and Families, U.S. Department of Health and Human Services, PO. Box 1182, Washington, DC 20013. Phone: 202/205–8347.

- Conduct research, demonstration, and service projects.

This program was strengthened by the 1992 legislation reauthorizing the JJDP Act. The legislation expands existing basic grants for centers for runaway youths to include street-based crisis intervention and home-based services.

State and local governments, for-profit and nonprofit private agencies, and coordinated networks of such agencies are eligible as grantees under this program. In selecting grant proposals, the Family and Youth Services Bureau of ACYF awards grants on the basis of the applicant's ability to provide services such as shelter, counseling, and aftercare to runaway and other homeless youths and their families; to provide services at a reasonable cost; and to ensure that a qualified staff is in place.

Federal financial participation in each grant varies and may be as high as 90 percent. The nonfederal share may be cash or in-kind.

The Transitional Living for Runaway and Homeless Youth Program

The Family and Youth Services Bureau of ACYF also administers this program,

Table 35. OJJDP FY 1992 and FY 1993 Discretionary Program Priorities

Program	FY 1992 Funding	FY 1993 Funding
▪ Comprehensive Strategy Targeted to Gangs and Violent Offenders	$3,240,000	—
▪ Research in Handling Juvenile Sex Offenders	$200,000	—
▪ Gang Prevention and Intervention	$800,000	$1,200,000
▪ OJJDP/Federal Law Enforcement Training Center: Youth Gang Intervention Training	$400,000	$350,000
▪ National Youth Gang Clearinghouse	$225,139	$339,512
▪ Private Sector Options for Juvenile Corrections	$300,000	—
▪ School Safety	$250,000	$200,000
▪ Targeted Outreach with a Gang Prevention and Intervention Component	$400,000	$400,000
▪ "Schools and Jobs are Winners"	$150,000	—
▪ "Serious Habitual Offender Comprehensive Action Program"	$517,000	$600,000
▪ Juvenile Restitution Training and Technical Assistance	$200,000	$250,000
▪ Professional Development of Youth Workers	$200,000	$200,000
▪ Community-Based Alternatives for Native American Youth Who Have Been Adjudicated Delinquent	$300,000	$400,000
▪ Chronic Status Offenders	$140,000	—
▪ National Network of Children's Advocacy Centers	—	$250,000
▪ Advocacy for Abused and Neglected Children	—	$2,000,000
▪ Juvenile Justice Clearinghouse	—	$814,714

which was reauthorized in 1992. The program provides resources to assist homeless youths in making the transition to adulthood and self-sufficiency. Grants may be made to state or local governments, federally-recognized Native American tribal governments, U.S. territories and possessions, and nonprofit organizations. Projects were first funded in 1990. Grantees must provide matching funds equal to 10 percent of the total project cost.

The Anti-Drug Abuse Act of 1988

Drug Abuse Prevention and Education Programs Relating to Youth Gangs

This program, administered by the Administration for Children, Youth and Families, is intended to prevent and reduce the participation of youths in gangs that engage in illicit drug-related activities, promote involvement of youths in lawful activities, and prevent chemical dependency among youths. Funds under the program support coordination of activities of local police departments, education, employment, and social service agencies; provide information on the treatment and rehabilitation options available to youths; coordinate support between schools and state and federal governments; and provide technical assistance to eligible organizations.

Eligible entities include state and local governments, federally-recognized Native American tribal governments, U.S. territories and possessions, public and nonprofit private agencies, organizations (including community-based organizations with demonstrated experience in the field), institutions, and individuals. Priority is given to applicants who propose to carry out projects and activities in geographic areas in which frequent and

The Anti-Drug Abuse Act of 1988: A Summary

Nature of Program

1. *Drug Abuse Prevention and Education Programs Relating to Youth Gangs:* Funds local programs to prevent and reduce participation of youths in gangs that engage in illicit drug-related activities.

2. *Drug Abuse Prevention Program for Runaway and Homeless Youth:* Funds local programs to prevent drug abuse among runaway and homeless youths and their families.

Funding Type

Yearly appropriation for each program. For the Drug Abuse Prevention Program for Runaway and Homeless Youth, a 25 percent nonfederal match is required.

For More Information

Family and Youth Services Bureau, Administration for Children, Youth and Families, U.S. Department of Health and Human Services, P.O. Box 1182, Washington, DC 20013. Phone: 202/205–8347.

severe drug-related crimes are committed by gangs whose membership is composed primarily of youths, and to projects that demonstrate the broad support of community organizations.

Drug Abuse Prevention Program for Runaway and Homeless Youth

This program, also administered by the Administration for Children, Youth, and Families, expands and improves drug abuse prevention services to runaway and homeless youths and their families. Services offered through the program's demonstration and service delivery projects may include individual, family, and group counseling; peer counseling; community education activities including outreach services; information and training; and improved

coordination of local services.

Grantees may be state and local governments, federally-recognized Indian tribal governments, U.S. territories and possessions, public and private nonprofit agencies, organizations, and institutions. Priority is given to agencies and organizations that have experience in providing services to runaway and homeless youths. A 25 percent nonfederal match of cash or in-kind contribution is required.

Summary

Table 36 outline each of the juvenile justice programs described in this chapter and their appropriations history for FY 1992, FY 1993, and FY 1994.

Table 36. Recent Funding History of Juvenile Justice Programs

Program	Appropriations (in millions of dollars)		
	FY 1992	FY 1993	FY 1994
The Juvenile Justice and Delinquency Prevention Act			
State Formula Grants	$50.75	$51.10	$59.50
Special Emphasis Programs	$18.10	$18.30	$21.30
Juvenile Gangs and Drug Trafficking Program	$3.50	$4.00	$5.00
Missing Children's Assistance Program	$8.50	$8.47	$14.50
The Runaway and Homeless Youth Act			
Runaway and Homeless Youth Program	$35.75	$35.10	$36.10
Transitional Living for Runaway and Homeless Youth	$12.00	$11.80	$12.20
The Anti-Drug Abuse Act of 1988			
Drug Abuse Prevention and Education Programs Relating to Youth Gangs	$10.94	$10.60	$10.60
Drug Abuse Prevention Program for Runaway and Homeless Youth	$15.29	$14.60	$14.60

Chapter 13
Federal Funding for Educational Services

Major sources of federal funding for educational programs are Chapter 1 of the Elementary and Secondary Education Act of 1965 (ESEA), Head Start, and P.L. 94-142, the Individuals with Disabilities Education Act (IDEA). Chapter 1 of ESEA provides funding for a variety of educational programs offered by both public schools and private agencies that provide educational services. Head Start focuses on preparing preschool children for academic success. IDEA addresses the needs of four groups of children: (1) school-age children with disabilities; (2) preschoolers, ages three to five, who have developmental disabilities; (3) infants and toddlers, ages birth to three, who are or may be developmentally delayed; and (4) children with serious emotional disturbances.

Education Programs under Chapter 1 of the Elementary and Secondary Education Act

Chapter 1 of the Elementary and Secondary Education Act funds three major types of programs: (1) grants to local education agencies (LEAs) for the education of disadvantaged children; (2) grants to state agencies for the education of migrant, handicapped, neglected, or delinquent children; and (3) Even Start grants for the joint education of disadvantaged young children and their parents who do not have a high school diploma. Chapter 1 also includes aid programs for state administration, evaluation, technical assistance, and program improvement.

Local Education Agency (LEA) Grants

The LEA grant programs of Chapter 1 serve educationally disadvantaged children from preschool through high school who attend public and private schools, including residential treatment centers with educational programs. Services funded by this program must be designed to meet the special educational needs of children whose academic achievement is below the level appropriate to their age. The program is administered by the Office of Elementary and Secondary Education of the U.S. Department of Education and by state educational agencies (SEAs) and local educational agencies (LEAs). There are no state or local matching requirements for Chapter 1 programs.

Most children served through Chapter 1 programs receive supplementary instruction in reading (74 percent); almost half (46 percent) receive mathematics instruction. In 1987, 4.7 million children participated in this program. Students typically receive Chapter 1 instruction outside the regular classroom, frequently during the time that other students receive classroom instruction in the same subjects, but a growing number of students receive Chapter 1 instruction in a regular classroom setting.

All funds received as Chapter 1 LEA grants may be combined and used for a single purpose at the local level. LEA funds are allocated, however, under two separate formulas. The basic grant formula allocates funds to LEAs on the basis of a

Chapter 1 of the Elementary and Secondary Education Act: A Summary

Nature of Program

Provides funding for educational activities through grants to local education agencies for the education of disadvantaged children, the education of children who are neglected or delinquent and living in state-operated facilities, and joint educational programs for children and their parents (Even Start).

Funding Type

Yearly appropriation.

For More Information

Compensatory Education Programs, Office of Elementary and Secondary Education, DOED, 400 Maryland Avenue, SW, Room 2043, Washington, DC 20202-6132. Phone: 202/401–1682.

count of children ages five to 17 whose families have an income below the federal poverty line; whose families receive Aid to Families with Dependent Children payments in excess of the poverty level for a family of four; or who live in local facilities for children who are neglected or delinquent. The number of children within these categories is then multiplied by a complicated cost factor: the state average per-pupil expenditure for public elementary and secondary education (which may be no more than 120 percent and no less than 80 percent of the national average), which is then further multiplied by .4. Since grants have not been fully funded at the level indicated by the formula since FY 1966, funds are reduced proportionately, but no LEA receives less than 85 percent of its grant for the previous year. Most Chapter 1 LEA grants are allocated under the basic grant formula.

The second formula—the concentration grant formula—is similar to the basic grants formula except funds are allocated only to LEAs in counties where the number of children counted in the basic grant formula for the previous year is at least 6,500 children or at least 15 percent of the total population aged five to 17.

Within the LEAs, funds are allocated to the school attendance areas with the greatest number or largest percentage of children from low-income families. In these target attendance areas, the most educationally disadvantaged children are served, regardless of their individual family income or whether they attend public or private schools.

The State Agency Neglected and Delinquent Education Program

This Chapter 1 program, administered by the Office of Elementary and Secondary Education of the Department of Education and by state educational and other agencies, provides grants to state educational and other agencies for the education of children and youths (through age 21) who are neglected or delinquent and living in facilities, including adult correctional institutions, for which state agencies (as opposed to local educational agencies) are responsible. Services provided under Chapter 1 are considered a supplement to basic educational programs funded by the state. Programs may be conducted directly by the state agencies or through contracts with local agencies or private nonprofit organizations. Up to 10 percent of each state's grant may be used for services to facilitate the transition of students from state agency programs to regular local elementary and secondary schools.

Grants are made to the states in proportion to the number of children and youths in state agency programs for children who are neglected and delinquent, multiplied by the same cost factor used for the basic grant program [the state average per-pupil expenditure for public elementary and secondary education (which may be no more than 120 percent and no less than 80 percent of the national average) multiplied by .4]. If grants are not fully funded at the level indicated by this formula, as has been the case in recent years, funds are reduced proportionately to the level of available appropriations. A state or local match is not required.

Even Start

This program is administered by the Office of Elementary and Secondary Education of the U.S. Department of Education and by state and local educational agencies. Under the Even Start program, the U.S. Secretary of Education makes grants to local educational agencies (LEAs) for joint programs of education for educationally disadvantaged children ages one to seven and their parents. To be eligible, children must reside in a school attendance area in which a Chapter 1 basic grant program is conducted and parents must be eligible to be served under the Adult Education Act (AEA); that is, the parent is not enrolled in school and is not a high school graduate.

The services provided under the Even Start program may include: identification of eligible participants; testing and counseling; adult literacy training; train-ing of parents to aid in the education of their children; support services, such as child care and transportation, when unavailable from other sources; home-based education of parents and children; staff training; and coordination with other federal programs, such as the AEA and Head Start. The federal share of program costs is limited to 90 percent in the first year of operation and declines to 60 percent for the fourth year.

In any year in which appropriations for the Even Start program are less than $50 million, grants are to be made directly to LEAs by the Secretary of the U.S. Department of Education. If appropriations equal or exceed $50 million, the Even Start grants are made to the states in proportion to Chapter 1 basic grants but with a state minimum generally set at the greater of 0.5 percent of all grants or $250,000. LEA grantees are selected by state educational agencies.

Grant recipients for Even Start are selected through a review panel consisting of an early childhood education specialist, an adult education special-

Table 37. Funding Histories of Chapter I Programs

Fiscal Year	LEA Grants	(in millions of dollars) Neglected/Delinquent Services	Even Start
1988	$3.8	$32.6	Not in operation
1989	$4.0	$31.6	$14.8
1990	$4.4	$32.8	$24.2
1991	$5.0	$36.1	$49.8
1992	$6.1	$36.1	$70.0
1993	$6.1	$35.4	$89.3
1994	$6.3	$35.4	$91.4

ist, and other educational specialists. Even Start programs may not receive grants for more than four years and must be independently evaluated. The Secretary of Education is required to submit a summary and review of Even Start program evaluations to Congress by September 30, 1993.

Table 37 provides the funding history for each of the Chapter 1 programs discussed here.

Head Start

Head Start is designed to improve the social competence, learning skills, and health and nutritional status of low-income children so that they may begin school on an equal basis with their peers. It is administered by the Administration for Children and Youth in the U.S. Department of Health and Human Services.

Services

Services available through Head Start to low-income children ages from birth to five years and their families include cognitive and language development; medical and dental services, including screening and immunizations; mental health services; nutritional services; and social services. Parents are encouraged to participate in the services that children receive through Head Start.

Eligibility

At least 90 percent of the children enrolled in Head Start must come from families with incomes at or below 100 percent of the federal poverty level. At least 10 percent of the enrollment slots in each state must be available for children with disabilities. The majority of children in Head Start programs come from families who are AFDC-eligible, families with very low incomes, families in which a parent is unemployed, and single-parent households.

Children Served by Head Start

Children enrolled in Head Start are primarily between the ages of three and five; most are four years old. Table 38 summarizes the age and characteristics of children enrolled in Head Start.

Head Start: A Summary

Nature of Program
An educational and nutritional program for low-income children primarily three to five years old that provides services to enable children to begin school on an equal basis with their higher-income peers.
Funding Type
Yearly appropriation.
For More Information
Administration for Children, Youth and Families/Head Start, DHHS, P.O. Box 1182, Washington, DC 20013. Phone: 202/205–8347.

Special Features

Head Start has three distinctive features:

1. *Parental Involvement.* Parents are encouraged to participate in Head Start as volunteers, teachers, and advocates for their children. In FY 1989, more than one-third of the staff of Head Start were parents of current and former Head Start children. Fifty percent of the members of the policy council for each Head Start program must be Head Start parents.

2. *Community Involvement.* Head Start seeks a diversity of sponsors, including community action agencies, incorporated agencies that serve only Head Start, sororities, school boards, and churches.

3. *Comprehensive Programming.* Head Start is designed to meet the needs of children and families in a comprehensive manner. Services must include not only early childhood education but also housing, health care, and family counseling.

Head Start Legislation

Three major pieces of recent legislation shape the Head Start program: The Augustus F. Hawkins Human Services Reauthorization Act of 1990, the Head Start Improvement Act of 1992, and the Human Services Reauthorization Act of 1994.

The Augustus F. Hawkins Human Services Reauthorization Act of 1990. In 1990, the Augustus F. Hawkins Human Services Reauthorization Act of 1990 made several important changes in the Head Start program:

Table 38. Characteristics of Children Enrolled in Head Start (Percentages)

Characteristic	FY 1980	FY 1982	FY 1984	FY 1986	FY 1988	FY 1990
Children with Disabilities	11.9	12.0	11.9	12.2	12.7	13.5
Age						
Under three	0	2	2	2	3	3
Three	24	26	26	25	23	25
Four	55	55	56	58	63	64
Five and older	21	17	16	15	11	8
Racial/Ethnic Group						
Native American	4	4	4	4	4	4
Latino	19	20	20	21	22	22
African American	42	42	42	40	39	38
Caucasian	34	33	33	32	32	33
Asian	1	1	1	3	3	3

1. Funding was set aside to improve the quality of Head Start programs through such efforts as increased staff salaries, additional staff, improved facilities, and staff training. In FY 1991, 10 percent of the appropriated funds were set aside for this purpose; for FY 1992, 25 percent.

2. The Act clarified that full day, full year services may be provided in Head Start programs.

3. Funds were reserved under the Act for parent-child centers that focus on early childhood intervention programs for children under the age of three.

4. The Act required that each center-based Head Start program have at least one teacher with a child development associate credential or higher training.

The Head Start Improvement Act of 1992. The Head Start Improvement Act of 1992 made several additional changes to the Head Start program. Under the legislation:

- Local Head Start programs are permitted to purchase facilities with the approval of the Secretary of Health and Human Services;

- HHS is required to use regulations for the purchase and safe operation of vehicles used by Head Start agencies;

- Younger siblings of Head Start children are permitted to use the program health services;

- Local Head Start programs are required to offer parents literacy and parenting skills training;

- Quality improvement funds are guaranteed to all local 1993 grantees;

- Greater discretion is given to the Secretary to waive the nonfederal matching requirement to ensure that communities facing difficult economic situations are not precluded from serving additional children; and

- Increased monitoring of new Head Start programs is required.

The Human Services Reauthorization Act of 1994. The Human Services Reauthorization Act of 1994 reauthorizes the Head Start program through 1998. The legislation continues the previous legislative emphasis on quality improvement, specifying that 25 percent of new funds must be reserved for quality improvement activities including:

- Ensuring that Head Start programs meet or exceed performance standards;

- Ensuring that programs have an adequate number of qualified staff, and that staff are furnished adequate training, including developing skills in working with children with non-English language background when appropriate;

- Ensuring that salary levels and benefits are adequate to attract and retain qualified staff for such programs;

- Using salary increases to improve staff qualifications and to assist with the implementation of Head Start development programs;

- Improving communitywide strategic planning and needs assessments; and

- Ensuring that the physical environments of Head Start programs are conducive to providing effective program services to children and families.

The legislation also authorizes the Secretary of HHS to make a collaboration grant to each state. To quality for these grants, states must appoint an individual to serve as a state liaison between Head Start programs and other agencies that carry out programs that serve low-income children and families. The grants will be used to ensure coordination of Head Start services with health care, child welfare, child care, education, national service activities, family literacy services, and activities relating to children with disabilities.

To strengthen the parental involvement component, the new legislation requires Head Start programs to seek to involve parents by providing opportunities for parents to participate in the development, conduct, and performance of the program and by offering family literacy services and parenting skills training to parents of Head Start children. Programs may offer training in basic child development, assistance in developing communications skills, opportunities to share experiences with other parents, substance abuse counseling, or any other activity designed to help parents become full partners in the education of their children. Each participating family must be provided with a family needs assessment that includes consultation with the parents about the benefits of parent involvement.

P.L. 94-142: The Individuals with Disabilities Education Act

The Individuals with Disabilities Educational Act (IDEA), previously known as the Education of the Handicapped Act, contains four major components: P.L. 94-142, Part B, Part H, and the Serious Emotional Disturbance (SED) Program. Table 39 summarizes each.

The Individuals with Disabilities Education Act (IDEA): A Summary

Nature of Program
Funds programs for children with special educational and developmental needs, including school-age children with disabilities (P.L. 94-142); preschool children (ages three to five) with developmental disabilities (Part B); infants and toddlers (ages birth to three) with developmental delays or who are at substantial risk of experiencing such delays (Part H, also known as P.L. 99-457); and children with serious emotional disturbances.

Funding Type
Yearly appropriation.

For More Information
Division of Educational Services, Special Education Programs, Office of the Assistant Secretary/Special Education and Rehabilitative Services, DOED, 400 Maryland Avenue, SW, Washington, DC 20202. Phone: 202/732–1109.

P.L. 94-142

P.L. 94-142 is intended to ensure a free and appropriate public education to school-age children with disabilities. Its provisions primarily fund educational agencies. The major programs for school-age children funded under the act include:

- basic state grants for education;
- regional and federal resource centers;
- services for deaf and blind children and youths;
- early childhood education;
- innovative programs for severely disabled children;
- secondary education and transitional services;
- special-education personnel development; and
- research and demonstration projects.

Appropriate educational and placement services for each child are to be achieved through the use of an individualized educational plan (IEP) developed for each eligible child with disabilities. The IEP formalizes the goals, objectives, and specific special-education and related services to meet the individual needs of each student.

Table 39. Major Provisions of IDEA

Component	Children Served	Type of Service	Appropriations (in millions of dollars)		
			FY 1992	FY 1993	FY 1994
P.L. 94-142 (State Grants)	School-aged children	Identification of special needs, special education and related services	$1,976.1	$2,052	$2,859
Part B	Preschoolers (Ages 3 to 5)	Early intervention services	$320.0	$325.8	$339.3
Part H	Infants and Toddlers (Ages 0 to 3)	Early intervention services for developmental delay	$175.0	$213.3	$253.2
The SED Program	Children with serious emotional or behavioral problems	Innovative approaches to special education services and service access	$4.0	$4.1	$4.1

Part B

Part B of IDEA provides financial incentives to states to develop early intervention services for children ages three to five who have developmental disabilities. The maximum per capita allowance for an eligible preschooler with disabilities is $1,000. Funds are awarded to state educational agencies. Included within the services that may be provided under Part B are social work services in schools, rehabilitation counseling services, and services to help children make the transition to school.

Part H: P.L. 99–457

P.L. 99-457, also known as Part H of the Individuals with Disabilities Education Act (IDEA), was enacted in 1986. As originally enacted, Part H provided states with a five-year time period to plan, develop, and implement a statewide, multidisciplinary, coordinated, integrated system providing early intervention services to infants and toddlers who are developmentally compromised and to their families.

Part H of the Act provides formula grants to states to plan and implement comprehensive, coordinated services for children from birth to age three who have developmental delays or conditions that raise a substantial probability that development will be delayed. Most of the limited funding is used for planning and coordination activities. Part H provides limited funding for services; the funds are designated as the payor of last resort for services needed by infants and toddlers.

Fourteen service components, listed in table 40, must be included in each state's service delivery system.

To facilitate the process, each state must have an Interagency Coordinating Council (ICC) in place and designate a lead agency to assume responsibility for the program. Table 41 provides a list of Part H lead agencies by state.

Under federal law, Part H programs must serve children who are developmentally delayed and children with conditions likely to cause developmental delay. States have the option of serving children who are at risk of developmental delay. States are free to develop the definition of "developmental delay" for purposes of eligibility under Part H. Approximately one-third of the states have chosen to include within Part H children at risk of developmental delays, either because of biological factors or environmental factors.

In 1991, P.L. 102-119, the Individuals with Disabilities Education Act Amendments was enacted, reauthorizing the Part H program and making several changes in the program by:

1. Strengthening family-directed, multidisciplinary assessments in the development of the Individual Family Service Plans (IFSPs) for each child who participates in the Part H program;

2. Establishing new procedures to ensure a smooth transition for children turning age three from Part H early intervention services to Part B preschool special education services;

3. Enhancing roles for the states' Interagency Coordinating Councils (ICCs) and the Federal Interagency Coordinating Council (FICC);

4. Mandating studies to address the appropriate formula to be used in allocating Part H funds through census data, as is currently done, or through a "child find" system; and

5. Mandating studies to determine the financial and programmatic effects of including or excluding "at risk" children in Part H programs.

The SED Program

This program focuses on the needs of children with serious emotional or behavioral disturbance (SED). The program funds a variety of projects to improve access to services specifically designed to meet the needs of children with SED and to test innovative approaches to improving special education services for children with SED.

Table 40. Fourteen Service Components for Part H (P.L. 99-457)

1. Definition of developmentally delayed.

2. Timetable for all in need in the state.

3. Comprehensive, multidisciplinary evaluation of the needs of children and families.

4. Individualized family service plans (IFSPs) and case management services.

5. Child find and referral system.

6. Public awareness.

7. Central directory of services, resources, experts, and research and demonstration projects.

8. Comprehensive system of personnel development.

9. Single line of authority in a lead agency designated or established by the governor for implementation of:
   - general administration and supervision;
   - identification and coordination of all available resources;
   - assignment of financial responsibility to the appropriate agency;
   - procedures to ensure the provision of services and to resolve intra- and interagency disputes; and
   - entry into formal interagency agreements.

10. Policy pertaining to contracting or making arrangements with local service providers.

11. Procedure for timely reimbursement of funds.

12. Procedural safeguards.

13. Policies and procedures for personnel standards.

14. System for compiling data on the early intervention programs.

Table 41. Part H Lead Agencies

State*	Lead Agency
Alabama	Education
Alaska	Health and Social Services
American Samoa	Health
Arizona	Economic Security/Developmental Disabilities
Arkansas	Human Services
California	Developmental Services
Colorado	Education
Northern Mariana Islands	Education
Connecticut	Education
Delaware	Education
District of Columbia	Human Services
Florida	Education
Georgia	Human Resources/Mental Health/Mental Retardation/Substance Abuse
Guam	Education
Hawaii	Health
Idaho	Health and Welfare/Developmental Disabilities
Illinois	Education
Indiana	Mental Health
Iowa	Education
Kansas	Health and Environment
Kentucky	Cabinet for Human Resources
Louisiana	Education
Maine	Interdepartmental Committee
Maryland	Government Office/Children and Youth
Massachusetts	Public Health
Michigan	Education
Minnesota	Education
Mississippi	Health
Missouri	Education

*The Federated States of Micronesia and the Republic of the Marshall Islands are not eligible for this program.

Table 41 (continued). Part H Lead Agencies

State*	Lead Agency
Montana	Developmental Disabilities
Nebraska	Education
Nevada	Human Resources
New Hampshire	Education
New Jersey	Education
New Mexico	Health and Environment
New York	Health
North Carolina	Human Resources/Mental Health/Mental Retardation/Substance Abuse
North Dakota	Human Services
Ohio	Health
Oklahoma	Education
Oregon	Mental Health/Developmental Disabilities
Palau	Education
Pennsylvania	Public Welfare
Puerto Rico	Health
Rhode Island	Interagency Coordinating Council
Secretary of the Interior (BIA)	Education
South Carolina	Health and Environmental Control
South Dakota	Education
Tennessee	Education
Texas	Interagency Council
Utah	Health
Vermont	Education
Virgin Islands	Health
Virginia	Mental Health/Mental Retardation/Substance Abuse
Washington	Social and Health Services
West Virginia	Health
Wisconsin	Health
Wyoming	Health

Conclusion

This manual describes several sources of federal funding that social service providers may draw upon to enhance and expand services for children and their families. Each program may be used to meet specific needs.

Traditionally, the use of each program, much like the presentation of each funding source in this manual, has been categorical. Increasingly, however, communities are considering how programs might be integrated in terms of service delivery and funding to meet the needs of vulnerable children, youths, and families in a more comprehensive and coordinated way.

Integrated systems require human, financial, and physical resources if the administrative and service delivery functions of multiple agencies are to be coordinated. This realignment has been characterized by such terms as *flexible dollars, wraparound services,* and *decategorization.* But no matter what term is applied to the integrated approach a community uses, certain characteristics tend to appear in each system: collaborative relationships, comprehensive services, a community-based focus in service delivery, emphasis on accessibility of services, a family focus, and cultural, racial, and gender sensitivity.

Integration in service delivery and financing has been the subject of extensive study. No attempt was made to detail that work in this manual. A few preliminary considerations, however, are offered, based on the information in this manual. These considerations may serve as a starting point in thinking about integrated service delivery and funding.

When the funding streams presented in this manual are considered from an integrated perspective, three issues may serve as a preliminary focus: potential overlap in program eligibility requirements, coordination of services, and improved utilization of service providers.

Potential Overlap in Program Eligibility

Service accessibility is likely to be enhanced when children, youths, and families receive assistance in establishing eligibility for multiple programs. Providers, however, must understand how eligibility overlaps in order to facilitate access to a broad range of services. Eligibility is not always easy to define, nor is it always easy to determine how it overlaps among programs. In some instances, eligibility for one program will trigger eligibility for another program. In other instances, receipt of one type of benefit will preclude receipt of benefits under another program. In yet other instances, eligibility may overlap for some families, but not necessarily in every case or in every state. At best, only certain generalizations may be made. Overlapping program eligibility can serve as a starting point in designing integrated service delivery and funding.

The Aid to Families with Dependent Children (AFDC) program provides but one illustration of the complex relationships among eligibility requirements for several programs. AFDC eligibility is frequently referenced in the eligibility criteria for other programs. Figure 5 illustrates the eligibility relationships, based on AFDC, among several programs discussed in this manual.

Recognition of some eligibility relationships has led to efforts to streamline the eligibility determination process for a number of programs through the use of

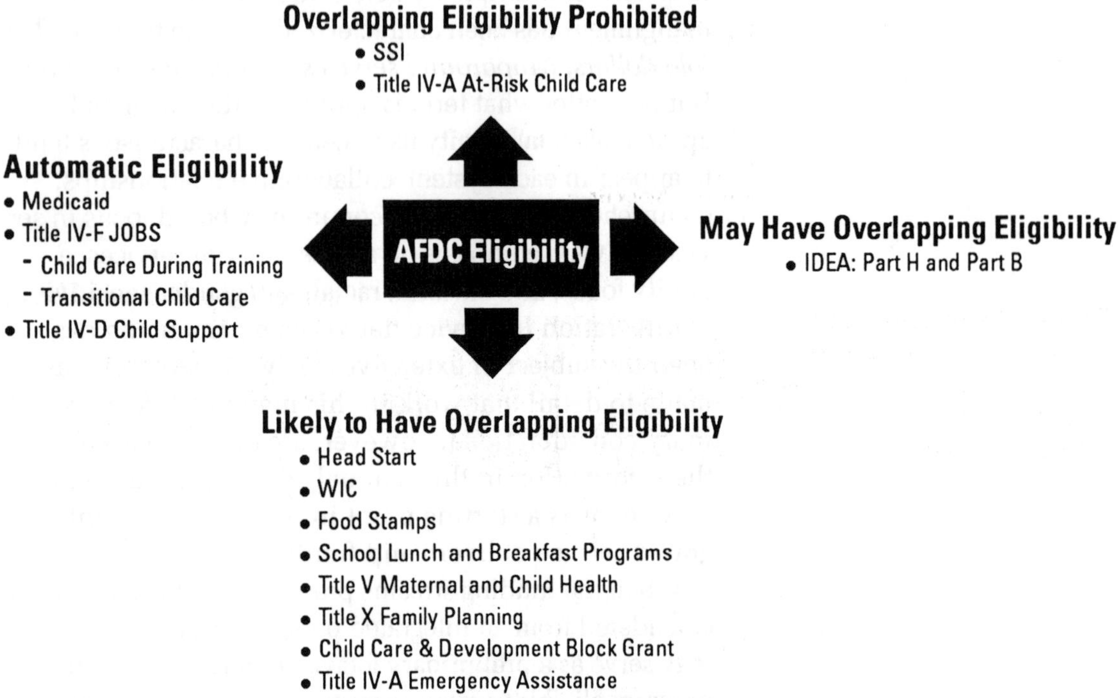

Overlapping Eligibility Prohibited
- SSI
- Title IV-A At-Risk Child Care

Automatic Eligibility
- Medicaid
- Title IV-F JOBS
  - Child Care During Training
  - Transitional Child Care
- Title IV-D Child Support

AFDC Eligibility

May Have Overlapping Eligibility
- IDEA: Part H and Part B

Likely to Have Overlapping Eligibility
- Head Start
- WIC
- Food Stamps
- School Lunch and Breakfast Programs
- Title V Maternal and Child Health
- Title X Family Planning
- Child Care & Development Block Grant
- Title IV-A Emergency Assistance

Figure 5. Eligibility Relationships

a single application. The U.S. Department of Health and Human Services, for example, proposed a model application form that states may use when pregnant women and their children apply for maternal and child assistance programs. The proposed model application encompasses Medicaid, the Health Care for the Homeless Grant Program, the Maternal and Child Health (MCH) Services Block Grant, the Migrant and Community Health Centers Program, Head Start, and the Special Supplemental Food Program for Women, Infants, and Children (WIC).

Coordinating Program Relationships

Coordination of services must also be considered from an integrated perspective. Service delivery can be coordinated to ensure that a comprehensive array of services is conveniently made available to children, youths, and families. There are many models for such a delivery system. By way of example, coordinating multiple services at Head Start centers illustrates a delivery system that draws on and delivers services funded under a variety of programs. Figure 6 illustrates how some of the programs discussed in this manual might be coordinated at a Head Start center site.

Coordinated Use of Providers

Finally, strategies to integrate services should consider the extent to which providers render services under multiple programs or render multiple

Health Care Services
- Medicaid Eligibility Determination
- WIC
- EPSDT Screening and Treatment
- MCH Block Grant Services
- ADMS Block Grant Services

Early Intervention and Development Services
- IDEA: Part H and Part B
- ADMS Block Grant: Mental health services for children

Head Start
- Educational services to children ages birth to 5
- Parental involvement

Income Support/Basic Needs
- AFDC Eligibility Determination
- SSI Eligibility Determination
- Food Stamp Eligibility
- Child Support Enforcement Services
- Title IV-A Emergency Assistance

Family Support Services
- Title XX Social Services
- Title IV-B Child Welfare Services
- Title IV-F JOBS Training on Site

Figure 6. Possible Coordination Pattern

services under a single program, such as Medicaid. Strategies may include streamlining the licensing, certification, or application procedures for provider participation in programs; developing uniform reporting and accountability requirements for multiple program areas; and developing reimbursement mechanisms to insure that providers are appropriately and promptly paid for the range of services they provide.

Summary

This manual provides an overview of a number of federal funding streams that may be of interest to providers of child welfare and other social services. It is intended to serve as an initial resource for basic information on a number of programs so that social service providers can effectively advocate in behalf of the children, youths, and families they serve and can access the funding critical to the ongoing delivery of the quality social services they provide. The current economic picture poses great challenges to the human services field. These challenges can be met with commitment, knowledge, and creative thinking. It is hoped that this manual will add to the existing knowledge base, provide a basis for planning integrated service delivery and financing, and support the commitment and creativity that already exists in the field.